The LOWDOWN on Families Who Get HIGH

Successful Parenting for Families Affected by Addiction

Patricia O'Gorman, PhD, and Philip Diaz, MSW

Child&Family Press

Washington DC

Child & Family Press is an imprint of the Child Welfare League of America. The Child Welfare League of America is the nation's oldest and largest membership-based child welfare organization. We are committed to engaging people everywhere in promoting the well-being of children, youth, and their families, and protecting every child from harm. All proceeds from the sale of this book support CWLA's programs in behalf of children and families.

CHILD WELFARE LEAGUE OF AMERICA, INC.
HEADQUARTERS
440 First Street, NW, Third Floor, Washington, DC 20001-2085
E-mail: books@cwla.org

CURRENT PRINTING (last digit)
10 9 8 7 6 5 4 3 2 1

Cover design by Michael Rae
Text design by Jennifer R. Geanakos
Edited by Tegan A. Culler

Printed in the United States of America
ISBN # 0-87868-873-0

Library of Congress Cataloging-in-Publication Data
Oliver-Diaz, Philip, 1948-
   The lowdown on families who get high : successful parenting for families affected by addiction / Philip Diaz and Patricia O'Gorman.
      p. cm.
   Previous ed.: Breaking the cycle of addiction : a parent's guide to raising healthy kids / Patricia A. O'Gorman, Philip Oliver-Diaz, 1987.
   Includes bibliographical references.
   ISBN 0-87868-873-0 (alk. paper)
   1. Alcoholics—Family relationships. 2. Children of alcoholics. 3. Parenting. 4. Alcoholism—Prevention. I. O'Gorman, Patricia A. II. O'Gorman, Patricia A. Breaking the cycle of addiction. III. Title.
   HV5132.O46 2004
   649.1'087'4—dc22   2004011879

Contents

Acknowledgments

No book would be complete without acknowledging those who made it possible. Thus we would like to begin by acknowledging the Child Welfare League of America's (CWLA's) understanding that a book was needed that could bring together those who care about children—both big and small—who come from families with many, many challenges, and for their support in making it a reality. Special thanks to Shay Bilchik, CEO of CWLA, for his support in publishing this book, and to Tegan Culler, for her wonderful editing. To Pat's cousin Billy Adcock, who provided us the title of our book on his final trip home.

We would also like to recognize the support we obtained from our families that allowed our long hours of collaboration to result in this product. From Phil's wife, Kathryn Brohl, for her understanding in the face of the chaos that this project brought to her home; to Pat's mother, Mary Mullen, who would accompany her on working visits to Phil and Kathryn's; to Pat's children who learned to "share" their computer (that is, until they obtained their own); to Pat's husband, Robert Ross, who supported her through the missed deadlines; and to our professional friends at the many institutes and organizations where we have consulted and lectured—we thank you!

Pat would like to acknowledge Phil for his vision in seeing the need to build bridges between child welfare, juvenile justice, mental health, and substance abuse, and for his support and ongoing friendship; and Ms. Rose Washington, for her vision in creating safe places for children to thrive.

And Phil would like to acknowledge Pat's leadership for her lifelong commitment to integrating substance abuse, mental health, and child welfare services; her determination to bring strength-based approaches to families; and her continuing love and confrontation over 25 years of friendship and collaboration.

We would also like to acknowledge the children, families/caregivers, counselors, staff, patients, and friends with whom we worked and who helped inspire the composite stories you will read. Although the details of their lives have been altered, their voices remain loud and clear and are an ongoing inspiration to us all.

Introduction

The Lowdown on Families Who Get High was written to address the needs of two groups of people. First, it is aimed at helping children of addicts, their caregivers, addicts, and their partners, on a personal level. Whether the caregiver is a birthparent, a member of the extended family, a foster parent, or even a professional child care worker or social worker, what all caregivers have in common is that they have accepted the responsibility of nurturing a child and safeguarding his or her well-being. But when it comes to addiction, most caregivers have little idea of the needs and issues facing children who have been affected by addiction, and even less idea how to help parents/caregivers who are addicts. All too often, caregivers are themselves untreated adult children of addicted families, or of families with abuse or neglect histories.

The book is also intended to provide greater professional understanding for those who work with addicted parents/caregivers and their children: child welfare, juvenile justice, and alcohol/drug-abuse professionals, who now need to collaborate closely—in some cases, for the first time. This collaboration will require a more thorough understanding of terms, the ability to identify and access services across systems, and the development of new services. With this in mind, Part III of this book offers information that will be useful to child welfare and substance abuse professionals and other helpers.

The Lowdown on Families Who Get High emphasizes the 12 steps of Alcoholics Anonymous, revised for parents and caregivers. Although it is not a replacement for the original 12 steps, this 12-step approach to parenting will help those working to, or those working to help others to, surmount some of the predictable hurdles that occur when one is trying to both to recover from the effect of addiction and parent at the same time. Based on almost 30 years of clinical work, this approach demonstrates to both caregivers and their counselors that being a caregiver and being in recovery can be a win/win situation.

PART I

The *Impact* of
Addiction

CHAPTER 1

Parenting with a
Drug Addict
in the House

I feel like I am drowning. I have three kids and a drunk for a husband. I never know what Dan is going to do next. He is great with the kids one day and a monster the next. No matter how hard I try, I can't get him to stop drinking or using cocaine. I used to be an honest person; now I find myself lying to everyone about Dan's drinking and drug use. Sometimes I think it would be easier if I were a single parent. At least I wouldn't have to deal with all the chaos Dan causes when he is drunk.

Last week we had a fight. It got very heated, and we said some very ugly things to one another. Later, I found my 5-year-old, Tony, hiding under his bed. Marcia, my 8-year-old, barely talks anymore and cries for no reason. Gina, the 14-year old, has been getting in trouble in school. I'm under so much stress that at times I take it out on the kids unfairly. I am trying my best, but how can I be a good parent?

Maybe Dan's right when he says he wouldn't drink and use drugs if I was a better wife and mother. I just don't know what to think. I feel like I live in the middle of a hurricane and no matter what I do, my kids are doomed to be damaged by both of us.

—Janet, 32, married to Dan, 36,
an active drug addict and cocaine user

The Impact of Addiction

Living with or being married to an addicted person is like living in the middle of a hurricane. Everyone gets swept up in the whirlwind of addiction. The spouse of the drug abuser often becomes as involved in the obsession with alcohol or drugs as the addicted person is, but for different reasons. Husbands and wives of drug addicts spend a great deal of time and energy trying to control the addict's behavior. Spouses often get caught up in a maze of excuses and lies in a vain attempt to hide the severity of the addiction from the outside world and from themselves. To keep from having to face the reality of the situation, they begin to accept more and more irrational behavior as normal for the family (Bepco & Krestan, 1985). Increasingly, the spouse of the drug addict or addicted person begins to accept that it's okay for his or her family to live in a chronic state of tension and stress. In fact, stress, tension, and unpredictability become the family's norm.

Janet is caught up in her own confusion and self-blame. She blames herself for her husband's drinking and drug use and feels like a failure as a parent. She has allowed herself to become overinvolved in protecting her husband from the consequences of his drinking and drugging, and in the process she has lost sight of what she needs to do to protect her children.

Parenting in an Actively Addicted Family

Janet can be a good parent, and she can limit the negative effects of Dan's drug addiction on her children. It will not be easy, but it can be accomplished. The single greatest problem that families of alcoholics or drug addicts face is that they let the addict set the ground rules, mobilizing around the drug addict's needs rather than the family's. The family responds to the drug addict's moods and desires. If the drug addict feels like going out to eat, everyone goes out, even if dinner is already on the table. If the drug addict is ill, everyone must be quiet. And the family must always protect him by denying the drug addiction and pretending that all is well within the family. The children sacrifice their needs to the drug addict in hopes of gaining his love and attention, but they are often abused instead. The sober spouse views herself as a victim of fate.

If the sober spouse is to parent in a healthy manner, this contract to protect and cater to the drug addict must be broken. The children must see that the family's needs are as important as the drug addict's and that they have rights and privileges just as their parents do. The sober spouse must become a role model of self-assertion and independence and must give up the role of helpless victim. Living with a drug addict need not define the family, if the sober spouse is willing to take charge and set limits on the addict's ability to affect the family.

This is no small order for someone in Janet's position. She will need to accept that she cannot take charge overnight. She will have to learn a whole new way of being in her family, and she will need to accept that she will not be able to do this alone. She will need to learn to reach out and ask for help so she can learn about drug addiction.

Some Basic Rules for Learning to Live with Addiction

RULE: *Go to Al-Anon.*

Al-Anon is a self-help program for people who care about or live with an alcoholic. Based on the principles of Alcoholics Anonymous, Al-Anon is a place you can go where you can meet people who have learned how to live successfully with an alcoholic or drug addict. You will meet people who will help you learn how to detach from the addict. You will learn about the disease of drug addiction. Most important, you will be able to get ongoing support from people who really understand what you are going through and how to cope with it. It is a safe haven, a place of hope and recovery.

Children learn to deal with life by watching their parents. Al-Anon will teach you new ways to deal with life and with the drug addict so that you can become a role model of health and self-worth rather than a model of victimization and resentment. Al-Anon will help you to learn how to communicate positive messages to your children. It will give you the help you need to give up the useless attempts to control the drug addict's drinking and using and instead take control over your life.

RULE: *Take charge of your family. Develop consistent patterns.*

The first step in learning to live with someone else's addiction is not to let the addict control you or your family. Janet has let herself become an extension of her husband, and unfortunately, her husband has let himself become an extension of his drug addiction. His world centers on his need for alcohol and drugs. As long as that is true, Janet must not let her world center on him, or through association she will become an accomplice in her husband's disease. She must learn the Al-Anon concept of *detachment with love*, learning how to love the man and refuse the behavior. The alternative is for Janet to remain merged with her husband in a continual downward spiral and having her children pulled down with her. She must learn how to support her children so they do not internalize negative messages about themselves. She must learn how to create calm in the face of the storm.

Be Consistent

Inconsistency is the hallmark of the drug-addicted family system. No one ever knows what to expect from the drug addict. One night he may be warm, loving, and extremely permissive, and the next night he may be irritable and unduly restrictive with his children. Children in a drug-addicted home never know consistent rules and therefore have trouble learning how to behave (Steinglass & Robertson, 1983). Planning is impossible if it is contingent on the addict's participation. Mealtimes, birthdays, holidays, or other events are always open to disaster if the drug addict is needed for success.

Studies have shown that the disruption of family rituals like mealtimes, holidays, and birthdays may have a direct effect on the transmission of drug addiction to the next generation (Wolin, Bennett, & Noonan, 1979). Make sure you set down rules for your children that are consistent, even if your spouse tries to change them. Plan mealtimes, holidays, birthdays, and other special events so that the drug addict is not a central part of the event's success. Make sure that your children can go to the movies or the amusement park, even if he doesn't show up to take them with you. It will be more work for you to take this kind of responsibility, but the payoff for you and your children will be worth it. This was Janet's experience:

> I suddenly realized in Al-Anon that Dan's drug addiction did not need to ruin our lives as well. Once I got that idea, it became easier. We had dinner at the same time, whether or not Dan was home. I didn't count on him to take the kids to ball games or on fun trips. We went on our own at agreed-upon times, even if Dan had planned to be there and failed to show up. The kids were relieved and grateful.
>
> I realized this was the first time in their lives that they could begin to count on anything really taking place when it was supposed to. Dan began to realize that we were going to continue our lives with or without him. He learned that we loved him, but we were not going to let his drug addiction control our ability to enjoy ourselves or plan our lives. The funny thing is, even though he hasn't stopped drinking, he is drinking less around us because we do not accept his drunken behavior anymore. And you know, he shows up on time for dinner more frequently. He even shows up now and then to go out with us when he's supposed to.
>
> The first time he didn't show up to go out with us when we had planned, we left without him, and I think he got frightened. The kids are feeling more normal all the time, and given Dan's drinking, that's a miracle. My self-esteem has gone up, too: I no longer feel like a failure as a parent. I no longer take responsibility for Dan's problems. It feels good.

RULE: *Validate your children's reality.*

Children from drug-addicted families are constantly forced to deny their reality. This is one of the most destructive aspects of growing up in a drug-addicted family. Most children in drug-addicted or alcoholic homes grow up learning to dismiss what they feel. Eventually, they can no longer tell what they feel and become emotionally numb. You can help your children avoid this problem.

First Step: Admitting the Problem

The first step is to admit to yourself and to your children the fact that there is a problem in your home and that problem is drug addiction or alcoholism. It's not that the drinking and using parent doesn't love them, but that he just can't show it. Your children need to have you validate their feelings. If you do this, you will teach them to face rather than deny their reality.

Janet explains how she learned to validate her children's feelings:

> It wasn't easy to learn to help the kids with their feelings about Dan's drinking and my enabling. The hardest part was learning to tolerate my own feelings of being a failure when the kids expressed their feelings about our family. In the old days, my oldest, Gina, and I would fight when she gave one of her "Dad is sick. When will you face that?" speeches. But as I learned about the effect my denial was having on the kids and became honest with them, we stopped fighting and became mutually supportive.

It is misguided to try to protect your child from the fact that one of their parents is a drug addict and that the relationship between their father and their mother is problematic. They know something is wrong. Giving it a name helps them to be able to understand what is happening to their family and why. When you deny the problem, you isolate yourself from your children. When you admit the problem, you draw your children in closer to you and give them hope and a sense of security in the knowledge that at least one of their parents is healthy and unafraid.

Second Step: Educating Your Kids

Children feel responsible for the problems in their families unless they are told otherwise. It is a normal part of the developmental process for children to feel that they are the center of the universe and consequently responsible for the good and the bad things that happen to their friends, siblings, and parents. It is especially important for you to explain that they are not responsible for a parent's drug addiction or for problems between you and your spouse.

Children need a way to make sense of the world around them. As the sober parent, it is important for you to learn how to explain to your children, in language appropriate to their ages, the concept of drug addiction as a disease. You need to find ways to help them understand concepts like "drunk" and "blackout." Most children have no concept of what drinking does to their parent. They don't understand that when Dad accuses them of lying about a conversation they know they had with him, he truly doesn't remember because he was in a blackout. Or that when

Mom passes out, she is drunk, not dead. At the end of this book, we list books and other age-appropriate materials that you may find useful in educating your children about drug addiction.

Alateen, a self-help program for children of drug addicts, is an important resource. It is a place where your children can learn about drug addiction and get support for dealing with their addicted parents. They will meet other children like themselves and discover that they are not alone. The introduction from the book *Hope for Children of Alcoholics: Alateen* (Al-Anon Family Groups, 1980) describes what Alateen is all about:

> *Alateen, part of the Al-Anon Family Groups, is a fellowship of young people whose lives have been affected by drug addiction in a family member or close friend. We help each other by sharing our experience, strength and hope.*
>
> *We believe drug addiction is a family disease because it affects all the members emotionally and some times physically. Although we cannot change or control our parents, we can detach from their problems while continuing to love them.*
>
> *We do not discuss religion or become involved with any outside organizations. Our sole topic is the solution of our problems. We are always careful to protect each other's anonymity as well as that of the drug addict.*
>
> *By applying the 12 Steps of AA to ourselves, we begin to grow mentally, emotionally, and spiritually. We will always be grateful to Alateen for giving us a wonderful, healthy program to live by and enjoy.* (Reprinted by permission.)

Third Step: Protecting Your Kids

This may seem very basic, and it is. Too often children of drug addicts report being angry with their sober parent because they did not stop the drug-addicted parent from verbally or physically abusing them. All children deserve to be safe. It is one of their most primary needs. Trust and self-assurance are both built from safety. If children are not taught that they are not supposed to be abused, they will learn to accept and even expect abuse, and they may become abusers themselves. A parent who protects her child is a parent who teaches her children that they are worthwhile and valuable people. She also breaks the cycle of abuse.

It is not easy to stand up to a drug addict. But if it frightens you, think of how terrified your children will be if you don't. Standing up doesn't mean fighting with the addict. It means not allowing abuse to take place. It may mean leaving the house with your children when the addict begins to get violent. It means making sure your spouse knows that you will not allow him to abuse you or your children and that you will go to the police if necessary to protect them and yourself.

Set Limits on the Drug Addict

Too often, the sober parent does not go for outside help because she fears that a public disclosure of her spouse's drug addiction will interfere with his ability to make a living. Protecting the drug addict from consequences allows her to continue using and gives your children the message that they must protect the addict and not themselves (Cermak, 1985).

As a responsible parent, you can decide to set limits on the drug addict. This may take the form of refusing to let your children ride in a car with the addict when she is using. It definitely includes getting help for yourself and your children even if the drug addict doesn't want help. Setting limits on the addict also means refusing to allow her to get away with blaming you for her problems and manipulating you or your children with false guilt.

Set Limits on Yourself

Having a spouse who is addicted to alcohol or other drugs leaves the sober spouse with a true sense of abandonment. It is a natural reaction for the sober spouse to lean on her children to fill the void. But leaning on your children for emotional support puts an undue burden on them. Recognize that your children need to be able to lean on *you*, and find adults with the appropriate ego strengths for you to lean on. Al-Anon will greatly help in this area.

Sometimes, sober spouses put their children in caregiving roles in the family. This can range from a child who is "mother's little helper" to older children who take care of the drug addict when he is drunk or using because they have been told that they are "effective" at handling him. This also is a mistake. The family is where children learn how to behave as adults. If a child learns that he or she is only valued as a caregiver, then he or she is liable to become a compulsive caregiver as an adult (Wegscheider, 1981).

Being responsible for a parent also puts the child in a parenting-the-parent role. This is very destructive and should be avoided. It makes the child feel like a failure because he cannot control the drug addict. Even at a young age, children know that parenting your parent is not right, and he is also likely to feel shame for the parent and himself. It is this role of "little parent" that adult children of addicts most often report as the source of their bitterness with their parents (Woititz, 1983). Protect your children from your urge to lean too heavily on them to help you with your spouse. Find other adults to help you with these tasks. Even if your spouse never sobers up, you can avoid this with responsible parenting.

RULE: *Show your love.*

Children of drug addicts need assurance that they are loved. Often, they conclude that their parents do not love them or else they would not drink, fight, or threaten one another, and so on. When children believe they are not loved, they assume that they are unlovable, and this affects their self-esteem and behavior dramatically (Gardner, 1976).

The sober spouse, who is generally under the incredible pressure of carrying the load of the whole family on her shoulders, may mistakenly assume that the children know they are loved by her efforts to keep them dressed, fed, and protected from harm. Children are not that logical. They need tangible, constant affirmations telling them they are worthwhile and loved. This is especially true for children of drug addicts. They are insecure about being loved. They can't understand how a parent could choose alcohol over them, and they often believe that the addicted parent does not love them (Oliver-Diaz, 1984). They also tend to believe the sober parent does not love them unless he tells them so and shows it. This is not always easy for either parent. The sober parent is often too emotionally exhausted to give much to the children. The drug addict is usually feeling too guilty about her children to be affectionate and loving when she is sober, and often displays affection inappropriately when she is high.

It is absolutely essential for you to find ways to show your love. Giving hugs at night, reading stories to your children, or just saying "I love you" are wonderful and important ways to show your love. Children need to be touched with affection. When your child comes to you for attention but you are too tired to give it, explain why you can't give it. They will understand that you love them but you are tired right now. Let them know that the drug addict loves them, too, but that he is sick and incapable of showing his love consistently right now. We have found that the phrase *Love is present but unavailable* is a simple and powerful means of capturing this. If you are able to show your affection to your children, you will find yourself enriched and nourished by the love you share with them.

Janet found this to be true with her children:

> *It's been great. Since I've learned to be more conscientious about spending quality time with the kids, the whole house has changed. It seems calmer. I know I am. There are times I come home from the restaurant where I work as a waitress, and I'm exhausted. Invariably Tony will call me from his room and ask me to read him a story or give him a kiss good night. When I take the time and he crawls up on my lap and I spend time telling him how special he is to me and we hug, somehow I am renewed. I realize now when I feel my love for the children and show it, I get more strength.*

Guidelines for Recovery

It will not be easy for you to change your parenting while living with an active drug addict. It takes constant self-awareness for you to make meaningful changes. You will often fall back to old patterns, but eventually, step by step, day by day, you will begin to see changes in yourself and your children. The Al-Anon pamphlet, *How Can I Help My Children?* (Al-Anon Family Groups, 1979) gives this checklist for parents, which serves as a good guideline for parenting in a situation with active drug addiction. It may help you identify areas you need to work on.

Checklist for Parents

- Do I think of my children as people who have a right to my respect?

- Do I make them feel stupid, inadequate, or bad?

- Do I humiliate them in front of others? Or do I correct them privately, allowing them to maintain their dignity?

- Am I courteous to my children?

- Do I habitually yell? Threaten? Nag?

- How do I correct my children? Do I attack their character? Call them names? Lose my self-control? Hit them? Make sarcastic remarks? Ridicule them?

- Do I jump to conclusions, expecting the worst? Or do I give them a chance to tell their side?

- Do I make a big issue over small things? Do I have the same reaction to small problems as I do to big ones?

- Is "NO!" my favorite word?

- Am I consistent?

- Do I use my children to try to control the drug addict?

- Do I resent it when my children seem to love the drug addict more than they love me?

- If my child resents me, can I understand why?

- Am I more truthful with my children?

- Do I try to set a good example? Or do I expect more self-control from my children than I do from myself?

- Do I encourage my children to express their feelings and then help them to deal with them, or am I still so uncomfortable with my own feelings that I condemn them for theirs?

- Do I set realistic standards for each child's age or do I ask too much or too little?

- Do I make confidants of my children, burdening them with my troubles?

- Do I let them be themselves?

- Do I try to be tolerant when they make mistakes?

- Do I praise them as much as I criticize? Do I praise them in front of others?

- Do I really listen when my children speak? Do I try to understand the feelings behind what they are trying to say?

- Do I let my children know they are important? How do I treat the things they make?

- Do I apologize when I am wrong?

- Do I set limits on behavior and enforce them?

- Do I show my children affection and tell them I love them?

(Reprinted by permission.)

Summary

It is possible to set limits for the drug addict while learning how to find ways to have your own needs met. This means you will need to separate yourself from the addict's ability to manipulate you and your family to meet his needs. You must take charge of the family and create an atmosphere of consistency and security. Children need to be protected at all times from physical and verbal abuse. They also need to have their reality validated; they need you to admit that problems exist in the family. Finally, children of drug addicts need reassurance that they are loved: They need to know both that you love them, and that the addict loves them, but is not presently capable of showing it because he has a disease.

You can limit the negative effects of drug addiction on your children. You can parent effectively if you can learn to love the addict, but detach from her and separate your family from dependency on her participation in family life. The best place for you to get the help you need to learn to live productively with an addict is Al-Anon. Working the Al-Anon program will allow you to learn how to live for yourself. In Al-Anon you will find people like yourself who will be able to give you the support you need to help guide your family through chaos and into health and happiness. You will find true friends who understand how you feel and what you need. Remember, a pathway exists to help your family through the ravages of drug addiction. You are not alone. There is hope for recovery.

CHAPTER 2

If You Are a
Recovering Addict
and a Parent

I don't know what's wrong with my family. You would think they would be grateful that I've stopped drinking and using drugs, but all they do is complain about how little time I spend with them. It would be different if I was out drinking, but when I'm not home, I'm either working overtime or at an AA (Alcoholics Anonymous) or an NA (Narcotics Anonymous) meeting. I'm trying to build a new life for them, but they're not the least bit grateful!

> —Jesse, age 38, one year sober and the father of
> 10-year-old Michael and 15-year-old Leann

Like many recovering drug addicts, Jesse can't understand how his family could put demands on him when he is being so constructive. He doesn't realize that his wife and children need him to be a husband and a father.

Parenting Is a Learned Skill and Hard Work!

The 12-step programs have an old saying that if you take a drunken horse thief and he gets sober, you now have a sober horse thief. The same holds true for parenting. Getting sober does not guarantee that you will be any better at parenting than you were when you were drinking. It only lays the groundwork for you to learn how to become a better parent. As Wally G., a 15-year sponsor in Alcoholics Anonymous, once said, "When you were drinking, your car was in reverse. Once you put the cork in the bottle, you shifted into neutral. But only through the conscious application of the AA and NA program can you get your car into drive." Jesse's car is still in neutral as far as his parenting is concerned. Like many people in recovery, Jesse thinks that just staying sober should be enough for his family. He needs to learn that parenting, like sobriety, is a learned skill and hard work.

The Impact of Addiction

As the book *Alcoholics Anonymous* states, "Years of living with an alcoholic is almost sure to make any wife or child neurotic. The entire family is, to some extent, ill" (Alcoholics Anonymous 2001, p. 122). It takes time for a family to recover from addiction. Everyone in an alcoholic family is affected by the addiction, but according to Dr. Peter Steinglass et al., (1993), many factors affect the family, and no one factor can determine the impact of addiction on the family:

> First, the psychological and behavioral impact of alcoholism is often far greater for non-alcoholic family members than for the ones actually doing the drinking; second, the magnitude of alcoholism's negative consequences is often unrelated to the actual quantity and frequency of alcohol consumed, or the presence or absence of medical or addiction pathology; and third, the impact of alcoholism may be largely determined by characteristics of the family environment. (p. 10)

What is clear is that everyone in the family gets a distorted view of reality. But perhaps the most distorted view comes from the addict.

During your years of active drug addiction, you lived in a world of extremes and developed distorted beliefs about yourself and your family. False pride and self-will ran your life. Your world as an addicted person was one composed of lying, using other people for your own ends, and manipulating. Everyone had to focus on you and your needs. Most of the time your children were secondary to your addiction, and from one day to the next, they had no idea of what you might do.

Some Basic Rules for Making Meaningful Changes

For your children, the first real test of your recovery is to see if you have really changed. And for them, that means a lot more than just not drinking or using. For your children, real change means that you will be available to them to lend them support and guidance. It means that you will see them as a priority and make time to be with them, that you will see them for who they really are and not just as an extension of yourself. For children of drug addicts, *recovery means having a loving and secure home in which individual differences are respected.*

It will not be easy for you to change. Change takes time, and it comes in small quantities. In the early stages of recovery, your family may not trust that you will stay sober or that any changes you exhibit are genuine. This lack of trust may frustrate you.

Through practice and understanding, you will come to accept the time it will take for your family to believe in you and heal the wounds of the past. You will need to be the best parent you can be, *one day at a time*, letting go of expectations of rewards from your children and spouse. You must avoid the urge to make your family over in your new image.

To make meaningful changes, you have to learn new behaviors, new ways of acting and interacting. Just as it took repetition and practice to create a life of abstinence and recovery, it will take daily practice and self-examination to be a healthy parent. The rules that follow offer some guidelines for you to keep in mind as you begin to learn to replace old attitudes with new ones.

> **RULE:** *Remember that being a recovering drug addict is only one of many roles you have. To your family, your most important roles are spouse and parent.*

It is common for newly recovering drug addicts to either become workaholics in an attempt to recoup years of financial loss, or become fanatics for AA, talking or thinking about little else (Alcoholics Anonymous, 2001).

Like Jesse, many recovering drug addicts don't understand that they need to strike a balance between their roles as provider, recovering drug addict, and parent. Working through the AA and NA program becomes the recovering drug addict's primary purpose. In their enthusiasm at finding a new way of life, drug addicts often forget that their 12-step program must be incorporated into their lives if they are going to be more productive workers, lovers, sons, daughters, husbands, wives, and parents. If real recovery is going to take place for the family, then the focus within the family must move from the drug addict to the other members of the family.

> *If I hear one more time how the people in AA and NA have changed Jesse's life, I'll scream. Nothing has changed around here. He still doesn't spend enough time with the kids, and all he does is talk about himself and his recovery! It was better when he drank. At least then he wasn't self-righteous, and sometimes when he was feeling guilty, he helped with the kids.*
>
> —Sarah, married to Jesse, and mother of Michael and Leann

Jesse was furious with Sarah when she finally shouted these words. He needed to understand that he was focusing too much on himself and his needs and not enough on his wife and children. His constant discussion of his drug addiction was creating deep resentment in his family. For his family to begin to see meaningful change in him, Jesse needed to be more of an example of the programs of AA and NA and less of a proselytizer.

Parents in early recovery often need to learn the difference between *practicing* the program of AA and NA and *preaching* about it. It's difficult, but it can be done. You need to apply the program's principles to the way you interact with your children and spouse, not try to get them to apply the principles to their lives. If you set a good example, that will follow naturally later.

For newcomers in 12-step programs, learning a new way of life and finding new ways to parent can feel utterly overwhelming. In his first year of recovery, Jesse was simply overwhelmed by the demands of family and program. He could not conceive of a way to be a father to his children and deal with the stress of learning how to live a sober life. So he withdrew from his parenting role and left his wife with an unfair share of the responsibility for the children. Naturally, Sarah became resentful and his children felt deserted and concluded that they had done something wrong.

It was Jesse's sponsor who finally helped him find a way out of his predicament. Jesse's sponsor told Jesse that he needed to learn how to work the AA and NA program into his life so that he could be a better parent. Jesse learned that saying the serenity prayer when his 10-year-old got out of hand was as useful to him as saying the serenity prayer when he wanted a drink. He began to apply the slogans and steps of the program to his everyday life as a parent. He learned the difference between taking a break from his children and deserting them. He also learned that he was going to be uncomfortable at times, and that, no matter what, he could not avoid his family.

RULE: *Teach your children about addiction constructively, using age-appropriate explanations.*

Although you need to educate your children about drug addiction, how you do it is almost more important than what you say. You need to give information in a way that will not increase anxiety and stress in children who are already stressed. Children often get confused when their recovering drug-addict parent attempts to explain drug addiction and the 12-step programs (Oliver-Diaz, 1984). Recovering drug addicts tend to use esoteric self-help program language and concepts when trying to explain the disease concept of drug addiction. But concepts like recovering from drug addiction "a day at a time" don't make sense to kids. Telling children that drug addiction is "cunning, baffling, and fatal" will only frighten them. If it's done carelessly, or without using age-appropriate language, telling children they are at risk for drug addiction may cause them to panic. Children need to have things explained in their own language, using concepts that make sense to them. Trying to explain too much too early in recovery might do more harm than good to your children.

Your timing is important, too. Studies of children with a parent who has gone into remission from a serious illness show that the natural reaction is for children to distance themselves from any discussion of the illness once the parent is better (Rice, Ekdahl, & Miller, 1971). This is a healthy thing for a child to do. It allows the child to experience a period of safety and security in the knowledge that the parent is better. In their enthusiasm for AA, many recovering drug addicts may overwhelm their children with information and concepts that they cannot understand or are not ready to hear. It is important that you assess the potential effects of what you tell your children about your addiction, consider whether or not the child can make use of the information at this time, and decide what is the most constructive way to tell your children what you feel they need to know. Describe things in a manner that assures them that you are healthy and able to care for them. Emphasize that while you need help to stay better, you get that help in AA and NA, and you no longer need them to take care of you.

Remember, if you constantly focus on yourself as someone who is recovering from a disorder, your children—especially if they are young—will believe that you are not really better at all. They will exist in a high state of anxiety, waiting for you to relapse. Learn to talk about yourself in positive terms. Don't describe yourself as "dysfunctional" or as a "sick drug addict getting better." Your children will misinterpret your humility for honesty.

RULE: *Create a balance between your recovery and other aspects of your life.*

Learning how to achieve balance in life is a major challenge for most recovering drug addicts. Addicts are people who love to live in extremes. In any family, it is important for parents to share themselves and each other with their children. To accomplish this, recovering drug addicts have to find a balance between spending time with their family and their self-help program.

Louisa, a 32-year-old drug addict, has been married for 14 years to her husband, Ben, and they have a 13-year-old daughter, Lourdes, and an 8-year-old son, Emanual. She is two years sober, and for the first time in her life she has gained a measure of self-esteem and has a great deal of pride in her sobriety. Louisa cannot understand why Lourdes gets angry when she calls herself a recovering drug addict in front of her daughter's friends from school or why Emanual is constantly asking her if she's all right. Louisa feels even more betrayed and hurt when her husband Ben argues with her about how much time she spends on the phone with AA friends.

One aspect of recovery is learning to give clear and healthy messages. For addicted parents, this means expanding your horizons beyond your disease, as Louisa learned:

It's amazing. My 8-year-old stopped me dead in my tracks last week. He asked me why, if I was better, am I always talking about how sick I am. I realized that through my need to talk about my drug addiction in front of him all the time, I've been giving him the message that Mom isn't okay. Since I've become his mom again instead of Louisa, the recovering drug addict, he seems a lot happier and relaxed. I now go to as many AA meetings as I did before, but most of them are lunch-hour meetings so I have more time with the kids at home at night. I set time limits on my AA phone calls at key family times—homework, dinnertime, and bedtime—so I can spend more quality time with Ben. It has really made us closer, and neither Ben nor the kids have complained about AA.

Addiction and Emotional Life

Feelings are a way of reaching into ourselves and out to others. They are the personal coins we use in transactions with others. We can count ourselves as autonomous people to the degree that we are in touch with our feelings and able to give them expression. In healthy families, the adults help children identify what they are feeling and support the child's right to those feelings (Black, 1981). This is not easy for the person with an addictive disorder.

> **RULE: *Own your own feelings and allow your children room to have theirs.***

Learning to Survive Feelings

Feelings are threatening to the recovering drug addict. Chemicals and food have been used to anesthetize his or her emotional life. The expression of any strong emotion is considered dangerous (Gravitz & Bowden, 1985). Because so many people with addictive disorders come from dysfunctional families, they have not learned to identify their own feelings; instead, they have learned to dismiss them. The recovering drug addict is often on a parallel path with his or her children in terms of learning to express feelings.

Often, the drug addict reacts negatively to his or her children's expression of feelings because he or she does not feel adequate to respond. Drug addicts may have no history to draw on in this arena. Too often, the parent in recovery responds to any sign of strong feelings his or her child by attempting to put a lid on the child's emotional expression so that the parent's anxiety level will diminish. Thus, the child learns to dismiss or hide his own feelings or suffer the displeasure of his parents. This repeats the cycle of denial that most drug addicts went through as children. This cycle of denial of feeling creates resentment, erodes the child's self-esteem, and sets the stage for chemical or food abuse.

Louisa's father was a compulsive gambler and womanizer, and her mother was a compulsive overeater. Louisa never had a chance as a child to express her feelings. If she tried to express any anger, her father would become enraged and beat her. Whenever she began to express her sadness at her home life or disappointment with her father, her mother would dismiss her feelings by telling her things were not as bad as Louisa felt they were, and then give her sweets to ease her distress. This taught Louisa that sharing her feelings was not useful and that food is the proper substitute for parental nurturance. Louisa later learned to substitute alcohol for food.

Louisa became alarmed when she found herself filling with rage whenever her daughter cried or expressed anger. It frightened her to think that she might become violent with her children as her father had with her. After examining her method of dealing with her children's emotional needs, she realized that she had also adopted her mother's minimizing approach to Lourdes's expression of emotion. She realized that she had to become willing to deal with her hidden emotional life if she was ever going to learn how to help her child's emotional life flower. Louisa worked on becoming willing to open up. She went through a difficult time, but she used her 12-step program to get the support she needed and was able to learn that she could survive her feelings. In therapy she was able to feel the pent-up rage she had toward her father and mother and find out that feeling such strong emotions did not make her a bad person. She was able to experience the sadness of the child within her, and she learned how to give emotionally to the 8-year-old Louisa so that she could give to her own 8-year-old son Emanual.

Coping with Stress

Learn to recognize when you are under stress as a parent and take responsibility for developing coping strategies. Recovering drug addicts must learn to acknowledge when they need a break from their children and then find appropriate ways to reduce stress. Many recovering parents become overwhelmed and blame the child rather than taking responsibility for caring for themselves in an adult manner.

Louisa was having a hard time coping with her son Emanual's temper tantrums. She brought him to therapy because she felt her son was "endangering her sobriety." It was her reaction to her son's behavior, not her son, that was endangering her sobriety, however. Louisa hoped that therapy could fix Emanual so that Emanual would put no emotional demands on her. Louisa could not tolerate his emotional mood swings, which were thoroughly appropriate for a child his age.

With the help of her sponsor and a therapist, Louisa learned ways to cope with the stress of meeting her son's emotional needs. She realized that the lessons from her 12-step programs could help her deal with her son's anger, just as they had helped her stay sober. She learned that the stress of parenting could be managed if she used the tools that AA had given her, such taking things one day at a time, doing first things first, or using the phone for support.

Impulse Control

The *Oxford American Dictionary* defines an impulse as "a sudden inclination to act without thought for the consequences." Most addicted people have problems with impulse control (Silber, 1974). They may accept or leave jobs impulsively, or even get married on impulse. During your active addiction, you ate, drank, or used drugs on impulse. During this time, a lack of impulse control affected your parenting.

RULE: *Think before you act.*

As the old Native American proverb cautions, walk a mile in your neighbor's moccasins before you judge him. In other words, try to put yourself in your child's place before you act out any spontaneous impulse, whatever your intentions may be. Ask yourself what it would feel like to be the recipient of the act you have in mind. This slowing-down exercise will save you and your child much unnecessary distress.

Inconsistency is a chief problem for children of drug addicts. If as a parent, you make decisions for your family on impulse, your children simply have no way from day to day to predict what their lives will be like. If one night children can stay up and watch television until 2 A.M., but the next night they have to go to bed at 9 P.M., they have no guidelines for setting their own behavioral expectations. They can't determine what behaviors are right or wrong because the rules keep changing. Children also learn that consistency is not required or expected in their own behavior. This breeds all kinds of difficulty for the child in school, where rules must be followed and respected.

For the recovering drug addict, impulse control is usually still a problem. Children from families with one or more parents in recovery often report that one of the most frustrating aspects of recovery is that their parents still do outrageous, embarrassing things to them and that they can never predict what their parents will do next (Oliver-Diaz, 1984). As we have learned, security and predictability are cornerstones of a healthy childhood. If your child is still constantly on guard because you are so unpredictable or because they still fear that you will humiliate them by some thoughtless action, then you must take care to correct this aspect of your parenting.

It isn't just negative impulses that interfere with healthy parenting. Many people, especially those in early recovery, are filled with all kinds of positive, loving feelings toward family members after years of not even being aware of their existence. Often, after years of being ignored by one's parent, the child becomes the focus of attention and frequent public displays of affection. Because the recovering drug addict has such poor social judgment, especially in early recovery, he or she may embarrass his or her children by giving them these hugs, kisses, and other displays of affection unexpectedly in public places. Jesse's daughter Leann was especially upset with her dad when, in front of her friends at a high-school football game, he kissed her unexpectedly and told her how much he loved her. Jesse's intent was positive, but his impulse control was poor, and he did not think before he acted. For Leann, this behavior was just like Jesse's old drinking behavior, in that he did not consider how *she* might be affected. It is important to screen all impulses before you act on them, even when they come from a loving place within you.

The recovering drug addict often confuses impulses with actions and needs help deciphering the difference between feeling, thinking, and acting (Silber, 1974). At times, every parent has negative impulses toward his or her children, but the recovering drug addict often judges herself harshly for harboring ill feeling toward a family member. These self-judgments often lead to unnecessary guilt for crimes never committed. As a parent who is a recovering addict, you need to learn that guilt is only appropriate for negative acts, not negative thoughts. You need to learn that it's okay to think anything as long as you screen your thoughts and impulses and only act on the ones that seem reasonable and helpful to your children. Give yourself credit for the level of impulse control you do exhibit, rather than punishing yourself for having the impulse.

Remember, most recovering drug addicts are themselves children of drug addicts. If you are an adult child of an alcoholic (ACoA), you were probably raised in ways that helped breed the impulsiveness in your personality. Learn to view yourself as courageous for being willing to stay sober and challenge the past in order to make a better future for yourself and your family. Remember, feelings are not actions, and feelings do not have to be acted out.

Compulsive Behavior

The flip side of impulsive behavior is compulsive behavior. The *Oxford American Dictionary* defines compulsion as "an irresistible urge." This is different from an impulse. A compulsion is repetitive. It is also restrictive and rigid. Compulsions are hard things to break, as any drug addict knows. The compulsion to drink is the first major challenge that recovering drug addicts must face and overcome. But you are not out of the woods just because you have stopped drinking and using. There are many other compulsions that you will face as a recovering drug addict that will need to be challenged. The clinical characteristics of compulsive behavior are:

- restricted ability to express warm and tender emotions;
- perfectionism and preoccupation with rules, schedules, and order;

- insistence that others submit to your will and lack of feelings elicited by this behavior;

- excessive devotion to work and productivity to the exclusion of pleasure and the value of interpersonal relationships; and

- indecisiveness, and fear of making a mistake (American Psychiatric Association, 1980).

It is easy to see how one or all of these characteristics can interfere with healthy parenting. If you enforce compulsive rituals, your family will feel locked in and hopeless. In a home filled with rigid rules, children get the message that only the rules count, not people. The rigid application of rules is typical in families in which addiction occurs (Bepko & Krestan, 1985). One goal for the recovering family is to learn how to live with consistent but flexible rules, as opposed to the rigid rules that previously set the tone for the family. In that way, each member of your family will feel valued and secure. Then they will experience your house as a nest and not a prison.

Children need to be validated for who they are. They need to get the message that you love them as they are, not for who they might become. The compulsion to make your family over in your image will breed resentment in your children and continue the pattern of self-doubt and self-rejection so common in adult children of addicts. Learning to validate your children as they are is a major step in becoming a healthy recovering parent.

Finally, you will need to learn that people are the most important gifts in life. Drug addicts are people who don't know how to reach out to other people. Often, a recovering addict will hide in perfectionism or become a workaholic to avoid dealing with interpersonal relationships. As a parent, it will be necessary for you to challenge your fear of interpersonal relationships and learn to be with your children, rather than avoid or judge them (or judge them by avoiding them). In this way, you will learn to share in the joy you can have sharing life with your family, learning to live with love.

Becoming a Conscientious Parent

Examine what you are doing and why. Having an urge or feeling an impulse does not necessarily mean you have to follow through on those feelings. If you take the time to examine those urges and impulses, you will find that many of them are best left dormant and that new and healthy ways for you to be a constructive parent will become apparent. Becoming a healthy parent calls for self-examination. Being conscious of the outcomes of your behavior allows you to make informed choices concerning your parenting. Becoming aware of your impulsivity and compulsivity allows you to be a conscientious parent.

RULE: *Keep a child-centered, versus a self-centered, focus when talking to your children.*

This is not going to be easy, and it will take practice, but it is one of the major building blocks for healthy parenting. Always ask yourself when talking to your children, "Is this about me or them?" The recovering drug addict is a self-centered person (Alcoholics Anonymous, 2001). This is not bad or good, it just is. Self-centered people tend to see the world as an extension of themselves.

For instance, when her daughter Lourdes brought home straight As from school, Louisa's reaction was to tell her daughter how good that made her feel and how glad she was that her daughter was doing so well in school. She continued to tell her daughter that her good performance in school made her feel like she hadn't wasted her life because now Lourdes would be able to do the things Louisa could have done if she hadn't become an addict.

How would that sound if you were 13? Instead of making her daughter feel good, Louisa made her feel bad by implying that she was responsible for her mother's emotional state. By telling Lourdes how good she made her mother feel instead of reinforcing her daughter's own good feelings about her success in school, Louisa imposed a tremendous amount of responsibility on her daughter. Louisa should have been glad for Lourdes's sake, not because her daughter could perhaps make up for her mother's mistakes. A child-centered response, such as, "I'm very happy and proud of you," would have been far more appropriate.

Being Child-Centered

Recovery for children begins when they can see that their needs have become primary to their parents and that they are no longer responsible for making their parents feel good about themselves. One of the primary ways that all children from addicted homes are abused is by the premature responsibility imposed on them by their parents. If you think back to your own childhood, you will probably remember times when you felt imposed on to make your parents feel better. Your substance abuse was a reaction at least in part to that childhood situation.

A child-centered family is one in which the children feel that they are valued and respected. This means that you see them as separate people. Louisa's compliment was all about herself. As a recovering drug addict, it is easy to fall into old patterns of self-centered behavior. To break the cycle of addiction, Louisa is going to have to learn to step out of herself and develop ways of speaking to her children that are child-centered and ego-enhancing. Give your children the message that although they are separate from you, they are still the most important people in your life.

RULE: *Progress, not perfection, is the goal.*

Perfectionism is a major problem for most people who have an addictive disorder. It is particularly destructive to healthy parenting. In simplest terms, perfectionism is the constant demand to meet excessive standards that are unattainable. The perfectionist always has a gnawing doubt that he or she is not good enough. Perfectionists believe that they can win love and acceptance through performance.

Belittling and chronic criticism are symptoms of perfectionism. The perfectionist minimizes all accomplishments. The perfectionist cannot enjoy any of his or her accomplishments because no matter how good they were, they could always have been better, and the perfectionist will focus on the negative. All this failure in the face of constant striving causes depression, low self-esteem, and stunted emotional growth. The need to undermine and downgrade everything and everyone creates intolerable stress on the perfectionist as well as family members.

Marvin is a former cocaine user with six years of sobriety. His plumbing business is successful, and he has become a respected community member. Marvin's wife Marvela, an adult child of two drug addicts, is a nervous woman who is a recovering compulsive overeater. They have three children, Rasheem, 14; Quintara, 15; and Jamel, 8. Both Marvin and Marvela are perfectionists. Their house is immaculate. Marvela is constantly cleaning and rearranging the house to get it "just right." Marvin is the coach of his son Jamel's Little League team. Although his team has a winning season each year, Marvin is confused by the low morale and lack of enthusiasm his players have for the game. When confronted by some of the players' parents on how much pressure Marvin puts on the boys to be perfect, Marvin's response is to give a lecture on the virtues of excellence and the power of pressure to build character. Jamel recently became seriously depressed and began to talk about suicide, which frightened Marvin and Marvela into family therapy. In therapy they learned that Jamel's depression stemmed from the insecurity and stress that their constant demand for perfectionism created. They learned that their inability to be satisfied with anything that Jamel did led their son to question his ability to do anything right. The resulting feelings of failure led him to think about suicide.

Accepting Limitations

The path to health as a parent is filled with many imperfections. If you approach the task of parenting with perfection as an ideal, you will surely fail. Admitting imperfection gives you the opportunity to learn and grow and allows your family the same room for growth. Everyone needs to make mistakes to learn, especially children. Those mistakes should be met with understanding. Goals need to be attainable for children. It is in the successful mastery of skills that children build self-esteem. If a child hears the message that he or she is not good enough, the child may grow up without the ability to enjoy accomplishments. The only way to avoid perfectionism in your parenting is to learn to be less perfectionistic with yourself. Freeing yourself from the bondage of self-criticism will allow you to find new joy in each day and lay the groundwork for raising healthy, self-affirming children.

Making changes in old habits and learned behaviors is never easy. But if you apply the same willingness to learn and change that you bring to your 12-step program to your effort to improve your parenting, you will find the rewards more than worth the effort. Remember, willingness to try new behaviors is the key to developing a heathier family. Perfectionism is a major roadblock to growth. It breeds a defeatist attitude. As it says in *Alcoholics Anonymous* (2001), also known as "The Big Book," "We are not saints. The point is that we are willing to grow along spiritual lines. The principles we have set down are guides to progress. We claim spiritual progress rather than spiritual perfection" (p. 60). Temper your parenting with the compassion for yourself and your family.

Summary

Parenting is affected by addiction. If you are a recovering drug addict and a parent or parent-to-be, be aware of the following things:

Your role as parent is as significant to your family as your role as a recovering drug addict is to you. The expression of feelings is threatening to people with an addiction. They have often come from families in which the expression of feelings was forbidden or abused. As a parent with one or several addictions, you need to recognize that this is your problem, not your child's. You need to work on being able to tolerate feelings in your family members. Impulsive and compulsive behavior are both problems for recovering drug addicts. The parent in recovery needs to examine his or her behavior to assess its effect on his or her children. The disease concept of drug addiction can be troublesome to children if not explained in the right way. Recovering drug addicts should be careful in their use of AA or NA jargon in attempting to explain their disease to their children and take care not to make their children feel anxious or insecure.

Progress, not perfection, is the goal. The healthy parent and family is one that allows family members to make mistakes and learn from them. The healthy parent increases self-esteem in his or her children and offers a safe and secure environment. With self-awareness and discipline, the parent recovering from an addiction can be a healthy parent.

CHAPTER 3

Children of
Active Addicts:
A Chapter for Caregivers

They don't love us. All they do is drink and go out.

—Tom, a 17-year-old child of a drug user

When do we get a chance? It's always about Mom and her problems, never about us.

—Lynn, a 15-year-old child of a drug user

Dad, who do you love more, me or alcohol?

—Juan, a 6-year-old child of a drug user

Children of substance abusers (COSAs) are the lost children of the foster care and addiction fields. Neither field truly understands the impact of addiction on children and offers little in the way of support for the specific needs of children of addicts. All too often the parental addiction and resulting family crises are the center of attention, and the needs of the children are swept aside.

—Reid, Macchetto, & Foster, 1999

Common Issues with Children of Substance Abusers
Parental Children

How children survive the turmoil of growing up with one or more addicted caregivers has been the focus of much attention. The roles that children of addicts play in their families have been variously described as the hero child, the scapegoat, the lost child, and the caregiver. We have discovered that at various times, children of active addicts take on all of these roles. Generally speaking, the one thing that they share is that they are parental children.

In addicted families, the children are given the responsibility for taking care of the rest of the family members and providing emotional support for both parents. Although more than one child may share this parental role, it often falls to the eldest female.

Parental children lose their childhoods to adult responsibilities. This often causes depression and may lead to thoughts of suicide (Fitzgerald et al., 1993). Sometimes, however, these thoughts get directed outside and these children act out in the community, as anyone who has encountered such children in the foster care system can attest (Booth & Zhang, 1996).

These parental children are often extremely competent children (Kumpfer & DeMarsh, 1986; O'Gorman, 1994). They have resiliencies, such as social and problem-solving skills, well beyond their years. This is both a curse and a blessing for these young people. Of course, these skills can be used in prosocial ways, but as many of us know—especially those who have worked in the juvenile justice system— many of these competent children are competent antisocial gang members. Their leadership abilities develop in ways that cause them problems later in life. Even when these skills are used in a prosocial manner later in life, these children often become depressed workaholics who have little self-worth separate from their work achievements. Here's what Clara, a successful 38-year-old foster parent and the adult child of two alcoholics, had to say:

> *I spent my whole childhood taking care of my parents and my brothers and sisters. I thought I'd left that behind when I became a lawyer and was hired by a prestigious firm. But it seems I took on a similar role at work. Whenever someone at work couldn't finish their briefs, I took over. It eventually lead me to become a partner, but it also left me with no personal life and a feeling of incredible loneliness and exhaustion, which was exactly what I felt growing up.*

When these children are in foster care or living in residential facilities, they often become the "little helper." And they *are* helpful! Unfortunately, being helpful to their caregivers often means they are not getting the care they need, and they learn to value themselves only in relation to taking care of others (Sher, 1997).

This often leads to children of substance abusers adopting a caregiving role in marriage later in life. In many cases, they marry addicts or become addicts themselves. These children need to be encouraged to take on more age-appropriate roles and accept being taken care of, rather than feeling that they must take care of others. This is not easy. Despite the toll that such caregiving extracts on children, it also offers them a sense of value, often the only sense of value they have.

Moving from Chaos to Predictibility

> *When I was 14, my friend asked me to come to her house at five for dinner. I asked her how she knew it would be at five. In my home we never knew what time dinner was going to be, because my mother was an alcoholic and everything depended on her.*

—Lois at 35, reflecting on her childhood
as the daughter of an alcoholic

Addicted families are chaotic families (el Guebaly & Offord, 1997). Often, nothing is predicable except for the pain, disappointment, and confusion that so many children are forced to endure. Dinner is often at strange times depending on the addict's condition. Bedtimes might be at any time or not at all. Substance abuse, family conflict, or the absence of parental involvement often undermines the celebration of children's birthdays, holidays, anniversaries, and special events. Children of substance abusers rarely, if ever, experience protected holidays or special events that are truly nurturing, as a family crisis or some other aspect of addiction usually disrupts the event. Children of addicts need to be taught how to cope with the inconsistencies surrounding holidays and special events. Your role as a parent or caregiver is to ensure that the celebration of these events is consistent and predictable. Whether they are in foster care, in residential child care, or in reunified families, these children must have predictable mealtimes, study times, bedtimes, holidays, and birthdays if they are to thrive. Especially if the children are still in homes where one or more caregivers are actively addicted, it is vitally important for caregivers or family members to help create some order in these children's lives. Their need for structure is almost impossible to overstate (O'Gorman, 2001).

Nevertheless, be aware that children of substance abusers may rebel, at least initially, against any attempt to set predictable expectations. In homes with actively addicted parents, the children often have a great deal of freedom. They may make the rules, or they may be responsible for enforcing the rules as they wish or as they understand them to be. Understandably, many children are reluctant to give up this level of freedom and control. Remember, be firm, consistent, and predictable.

Substance Abuse as a Coping Mechanism

Families are where we learn how to live in the world. For children who live in an addicted family, the adult role modeling is dramatically influenced by drug use. Children learn that drugs are an appropriate coping mechanism, and drugs may be associated with the expression of strong feelings, including love. Children from such families, especially adolescents, may seek emotional expression, or to anesthetize strong emotions, through the use of illegal drugs (Kumpfer, 1999). You need to remember this when dealing with drug use among adolescent children of substance abusers. If you suspect that your child is using drugs or alcohol, seek professional help, or at the very least, take your child to a treatment center for an assessment.

Guilt

Children from substance-abusing homes often feel responsible for their parents' drug use. This is often encouraged by the parents, who may blame their children for the many problems in the family. Caregivers must continually state and restate that the children are not responsible for their family's problems. For young children, especially, who are still at a developmental point where they feel that they are the center of the world, this sense of responsibility is understandable, but older children experience it too (Natasi & DeZolt, 1994). Thus, it is extremely important for you to find developmentally appropriate ways to teach children of addicts the message, *"You didn't cause the problem of addiction, you can't cure the problem, and you can't control the problem."*

Shame

> *I lived in dread of anyone, my friends or teachers, meeting my mother. I never knew what she was going to do next. One time she went to work with her dress on inside out! She would often open the door to our house dressed only in a nightgown, and that was usually half open.*

> —Sheila, a 16-year-old child of an alcoholic single mother

Children from substance-abusing families often experience shame in relation to their parents' drug use and the behavior that accompanies the drug use. Shame is associated with the illegality of their parents' behavior, with the way their parents behave in public when they are out of control, and with the parents' inability to take care of themselves (Sher, 1997).

This is especially true as it relates to bodily functions of the parents when they are drunk or high. Children may be expected to clean up parents who have urinated on themselves or passed out in various stages of undress. They may be expected to sit with parents who are out of control emotionally and take care of them. These experiences are often deep secrets, filling the children with disgust and shame.

For children of addicts, humiliation may occur at any time, because their parents are totally unpredictable. These children avoid all possibilities of public exposure, keeping their parents away from school and their friends.

Secrecy

Above all, drug abuse is the family secret. Children are taught never to discuss the family's problems with outsiders. The family forms a rigid wall of silence. It is important to remember that these children will not discuss their families without first establishing a great deal of trust. Even when they trust someone, they may not discuss their families because of a very real fear that they will be placed in the foster care system. In a very real sense, the child has to betray the family to get help for him- or herself. Often, the child who reaches for help becomes an outcast to the rest of the family. If you are becoming a caregiver for a child of a substance abuser, it is necessary to show appreciation for the great sacrifice that these children make when they break the family secret.

Sexual Abuse

Alcohol and other drugs lower inhibitions. Therefore, children of addicts can be at risk of being sexually abused (Famularo, Kinscherff, & Fenton, 1992). Such abuse may take many forms. These children may live in a highly sexualized environment in which parents may talk inappropriately about their sex lives or are careless about the way they are dressed. Intentionally or unintentionally, parents may expose themselves to their children without thinking while under the influence. And during blackouts, parents can pose an especially dangerous threat to their kids.

The normal boundaries that exist in families are often missing. Adults may walk in on young adults dressing or barge in while their children are in the bathroom. In addition, children are exposed to their parents' drinking and drugging friends. When their parents are incapacitated by drug or alcohol use, their children can be vulnerable to molestation by these friends. Some parents may even barter for drugs by offering sexual favors from their own children.

Remember, children who have experienced inappropriate forms of sexual exposure or contact may be fearful or hypersensitive with regard to touch. They may also demonstrate sexually provocative behaviors. You may need to establish clear boundaries around basic personal roles, behaviors, and social norms, as well as help them understand that guiding them is not an indication they have been bad or done something shameful. It will take time for them to trust enough to feel safe and really know that they will be protected. As part of the process, they will see if you mean what you say by testing the boundaries you set (Brohl & Case-Potter, 2004).

Conditions That Might Indicate Your Child Has Been Sexually Abused

It is generally agreed children might:

- *Complain of pain while urinating or having bowel movements, indicating infection.*

- *Exhibit symptoms of genital infections, such as offensive genital odors, or symptoms indicating a sexually transmitted disease.*

- *Have symptoms indicating evidence of physical trauma (abrasions or lesions) to the genital area.*

- *Begin wetting the bed.*

- *Experience a loss of appetite or other eating problems, including gagging without logical explanation.*

- *Show an unusual fear of being in a particular area of the house or some other place. If a young child is suddenly afraid of the bathtub or his or her bed, it can indicate that something disturbing happened there.*

- *Wake up during the night sweating, screaming or shaking, or with nightmares.*

- *Masturbate excessively.*

- *Show unusually aggressive behavior toward family members, friends, pets or toys.*

- *Engage in persistent sexual play with friends, toys or pets.*

- *Have unexplained periods of panic, which might be flashbacks of abuse episodes.*

- *Regress to behaviors too young for the stage of development they have already achieved, such as thumb sucking or talking very loudly.*

- *Initiate sophisticated sexual behavior (not developmentally appropriate for the child's age) toward other children or adults. For instance, professionals can pretty well determine that if a four-year-old child is trying to insert his penis into the rectum of a two-year-old boy or girl he has learned the behavior from someone. Caressing another child's genital area may be another indication for behavior not appropriate for the child's age. Wanting to stick his or her tongue into the mouth of another when kissing, or wanting an adult to rub the genital area is an indicator.*

- *Indicate a sudden reluctance to be alone with a familiar person.*

- *Engage in self-mutilation, such as sticking themselves with pins or cutting themselves with sharp objects.*

- *Withdraw abruptly from activity with a club or group that was formerly enjoyed.*

- *Ask an unusual amount of questions about human sexuality (particularly older—seven and up—children.)*

- *Suddenly not perform as well in school.*

- *Show an unexplained change in personality traits. An outgoing, carefree child may become quiet and withdrawn.*

- *Develop an unexplained fear of males or females. Or of a particular way people dress.*

- *Make sudden requests for locks on the door and other safety precautions, and ask questions about protection.*

- *Express thought about death or suicide, or display suicidal actions.*

- *Develop an extreme fear of undressing in a physical education class or for a medical examination.*

- *Develop frequent unexplained health problems. Recurring stomachaches, headaches, and pains in muscles and bones that have no logical cause.*

- *Not wanting to attend school when this was not a problem before.*

- *Begin to abuse drugs or alcohol.*

- *Demonstrate exaggerated startle responses to sudden noises or loud sounds.*

- *Become obsessive with regard to rituals such as washing hands, counting, or wearing certain pieces of clothing or accessories.*

- *Have poor hygiene or develop poor hygiene.*

—(Brohl & Case-Potter, 2004, pp. 17–20. Reprinted by permission.)

No one behavior can confirm sexual abuse, but changes in behavior such as these may indicate abuse, and you should investigate the possibility. According to Brohl and Case-Potter (2004), "If you suspect a molestation, talk with your child in a non-threatening, non-accusing, non-confrontative way. Indicate your concern, interest, and support. Make it clear you don't think your child has done anything wrong. But give him or her the opening to say that someone is doing something that doesn't seem right" (p. 10).

Additionally, using a metaphorical story can sometimes elicit a disclosure from a child who would feel too overwhelmed by direct questioning. For example, you may share a story about a little deer that had something sad happen to her when she wandered into the woods. She couldn't tell anyone what happened even though they tried to guess. Finally, she met a kind angel who told her how brave the little deer was and how good it would be to "just get it out." Feeling much relief, the little deer told her family what happened. Children relate to stories with favorite characters and will probably respond within a few days if the story such as the one here is familiar to them as well.

Posttraumatic Stress Disorder: A Special Issue

Parents and caregivers of children of substance abusers should know something
about posttraumatic stress disorder (PTSD) and understand the needs of traumatized children. According to Kathryn Brohl (2004), an expert in posttraumatic
stress disorder:

> PTSD is an anxiety disorder that represents a cluster of symptoms children acquire over
> time to fight anxiety and depression. Their condition can lead to hyperarousal, aggres-
> siveness, avoidance behaviors, reenactment, hypersensitivity, and a score of other prob-
> lems. Other conditions in anxious children include the inability to speak in their own
> behalf, exaggerated startle responses, a feeling of invisibility, as well as hypersensitivity
> about being misunderstood. The core issue for children with PTSD is seeking physical and
> emotional safety. (p. 57)

In *Working with Traumatized Children* (1996), Brohl wrote that PTSD
"surface(s) when a child's hyperaroused state causes him/her: to feel as though she
is reexperiencing her trauma; and to persistently avoid any physical or emotional
associations with the trauma."

According to the American Psychiatric Association's *Diagnostic and Statistical
Manual of Mental Disorders* (4th ed., 1994):

> A person with PTSD has been exposed to a traumatic event in which both of the following
> were present:
>
> 1) the person experienced, witnessed, or was confronted with an event or events that
>   involved actual or threatened death or serious injury, or threat to the physical integ-
>   rity of self or others; and
>
> 2) the person's response involved intense fear, helplessness, and horror. In children this
>   may be expressed by disorganized or agitated behavior. (As quoted in Brohl
>   1996, p. 12–13. Reprinted by permission.)

It is important to be familiar with the symptoms of PTSD and know what to do
about them. Reactions to trauma span a wide range. They include rage, excessive
aggression, depression, numbing, panic attacks, avoidance behaviors, short- or long-
term memory loss, lack of concentration, feeling separate from one's body, developmental regression, compulsive behavior, and high-risk play. Other important
symptoms include flashbacks, sleep disturbances, somatic complaints such as stomachaches, and breathing disorders, eating disorders, and elimination disorders.

Just like sexual abuse, PTSD is affected by triggers that stimulate symptoms. Brohl
(1996) described possible triggers as:

- *Loud noises—yelling or cars backfiring*

- *Discussing about the trauma*

- *Feeling physically vulnerable*

- *Certain music, types of dancing, or works of art associated with the trauma*

- *Smells, textures*

- *Certain times of the day*

- *Anniversaries of events that may be connected to trauma such as death, accidents*

- *Exposure to weapons or things that might have been used as weapons*

- *Certain physical characteristics—beards, long hair—that may have been part of a traumatic event*

- *Sexual contact of any kind* (p. 11)

Recognizing the symptoms of sexual abuse and PTSD is only part of the solution for children of addicts. Knowing what to do to help is equally important. There is much that can be done to help these children, but the most important thing of all is to help them feel safe. If abuse is ongoing, inform the authorities and ensure that it stops. If abuse occurred in the past and the child shares it with you, validate his or her emotions about it by speaking to him or her about the incident. Validation means that you tell the child that you believe him or her; confirm that his or her feelings and reactions to the abuse are understandable, even normal given the circumstances; and that you will support the child throughout the process of sharing his or her story.

Guidelines

- Stay calm as you hear about what happened to the child. Remember, this is a time for her to feel safe in sharing her experience. If you become too emotional, the child may feel that she has to take care of *you*.

- Get as many details as he is comfortable sharing. If the child is uncomfortable communicating something verbally, have him draw it.

- Ask the child if she has told anyone about this before you. If you are the first person to hear this story, by law you must report the incident to child protective services. If the child shares with you that she has told someone else, verify that the report has been submitted. This will mean that you will need to call child protective services to find out if a report has already been filed. If it has not been submitted, you will need to report the incident.

- Ask the child how she feels, how long she has felt this way, and whether she has any other feelings about this (remember, she may have many different conflicting feelings).

- Tell her that it must be difficult to feel this way.

- Share that other children who have had the same experience feel the same way.

- Remember to refer to our list of triggers and our list of indicators for sexual abuse.

- If the child has a panic attack, help him to feel safe in the present, and let him know the feelings he has are from a past event.

The best thing you can do is to make yourself knowledgeable regarding sexual abuse and PTSD. Two excellent resources, on which we relied heavily in writing this chapter, are *Working with Traumatized Children: A Handbook for Healing*, by Kathryn Brohl (CWLA Press, 1996), and *When Your Child Has Been Molested: A Parent's Guide to Healing and Recovery*, by Kathryn Brohl and Joyce Case-Potter (Jossey-Bass, 2004).

Summary

Children in actively drug-using homes need help. They need to be able to feel that someone understands their plight, that someone is on their side and believes them. They need to be able to be children, not left in roles where they take care of the rest of the family. They also need predictability and order in their lives to offset the chaos of living with an addict.

Because the potential for violence or sexual abuse in a drug-affected home is very high, PTSD and sexual abuse are special issues for these children. Therefore, caregivers should familiarize themselves with the symptoms of PTSD and the indicators of sexual abuse. Some of the symptoms that caregivers should look for are the reenactment of physical or emotional trauma, bedwetting, fear of certain types of people reminiscent of abusers, fear of situations that remind children of trauma they witnessed, and somatic complaints such as stomachaches, sleep problems, and eating disorders. If you are a caregiver, you will need to teach the children ways to protect themselves from high-risk situations and help them protect themselves from the always-present threat of a flashback to less safe times.

Just knowing that a supportive adult is available is very helpful for children living with active addicts. But it is not a job to take lightly once you make yourself available to one of these children. You need to demonstrate that you are different than the addict and that you are there for the child when she or he needs you.

CHAPTER 4

A Child's View of
Recovery

I don't care if I get in trouble. I'd do it again. Nobody cares about me. I'm invisible.

—10-year-old Lance, the son of Walter,
a recovering alcoholic, and Wendy,
the adult daughter of two alcoholics

Negotiating Recovery

Lance was caught stealing by Ms. Lewis, the school social worker. He had taken something from another student's desk. Ms. Lewis, who knew about Lance's father and had helped Lance when his father was actively drinking, questioned Lance. Later, she admitted painfully:

> *I couldn't believe it. There was Lance in trouble for stealing again. I understood why Lance got into trouble when his father was drinking—I spent many an hour counseling Lance then. But I thought everything would be fine now that his father was sober. Now after talking to him, I'm not so sure anymore. I've never spoken to such a confused little boy before.*
>
> *He told me with his eyes full of tears that he lost his best friend when his dad got sober. When I asked him who that was, he said, breaking out in tears, "You! You don't care about me anymore!" I realized that once his father had become sober, I had withdrawn from Lance, and that the only way for him to get my attention back was to get into trouble*

again. I realize now that he was very ambivalent about his father and that he still needed help from me to negotiate his father's sobriety, just like we had negotiated his drunken-ness. I realized that in some ways this little boy was more isolated now that his parents were in recovery programs than he was before they went for help. He was mourning many things, including our relationship.

It is not easy for children of alcoholics to negotiate their parents' recovery. It can be a very confusing time, especially for young children. Change is scary, especially to children from chaotic homes. Children need help to make sense of all the changes that take place in a family that is recovering from alcoholism. As a parent, you must consider many things to help your children negotiate your family's recovery from addiction. As Lance's mom, Wendy, learned:

> *I couldn't believe that Lance was stealing when his teacher called to let me know. He had always been a responsible child and a great help to me when Walter was drinking. It was hard to believe that now that Walter was sober, Lance would be caught stealing. It wasn't until I spoke to the school social worker that I understood how confused Lance was and how much help he needed to adjust to the changes in our family. Once Walter and I understood what he needed, we were able to help, and Lance calmed down.*

One of the things that Wendy and Walter did to help Lance was to explain to him what was happening to his family. They helped the boy sort out the many things that were upsetting him.

Things That Frighten or Confuse

Hospitals are scary places for children. Children often have very negative fantasies about hospitals and need to be reassured that their parents are okay. If a parent was hospitalized, your children would need to understand what happened in the hospital. This is particularly true for children of alcoholic parents. Often, a parent returning from an alcoholism treatment program acts and seems very different to the children. And indeed, if the treatment was successful, the parent has changed in some very important ways. This "new" parent is often confusing to the child, however. The children need to have the hospitalization explained in a manner appropriate to their ages.

Children may also be confused when a parent joins a self-help group like Alcoholics Anonymous. Children have all kinds of unanswered questions during the early stages of recovery from alcoholism, and they need guidance. Children need help understanding where their parents go at night and why. They may also have very mixed feelings about their family changing. If Mom and Dad have developed a new closeness, they may feel jealous. There is a period of adjustment to a newly

sober parent that children may find extremely difficult. For example, if newly sober Dad takes a more active role in setting limits on them, they may decide that he
was better drunk.

Finally, children need to find out where they fit in this newly reconstructed
family. They need a parent or caregiver to help them negotiate this very difficult
time. Lance lost his best friend when his dad got sober because his best friend thought
she wasn't needed anymore. Parents can make this mistake, too. They believe that
they are not needed as much because the drinking has stopped. They do not realize
that in many ways, they are needed more, not less. As parents, you need to realize
that early recovery is a time of change and confusion for your whole family. Even
positive change creates anxiety in your children, and they need your support.

The Chemical Is Not the Issue

> *I wish my father could realize he is an alcoholic and go for help!*

> —Antonia, a 16-year-old in a children-of-alcoholics group

> *Why? My father stopped drinking and went to AA, but he's no better.*

> —Sandy, a 15-year-old in the same group

From the child's point of view, parental drinking is not the issue. For Lance's sister
Sandy, getting better means a lot more than not drinking:

> *It wasn't always bad for me and my brother Lance when Dad drank. Sometimes Dad was*
> *real nice when he drank, and bought us gifts and things. I'm glad Dad stopped drinking*
> *because now we have more money, and I don't find him passed out anymore. But many*
> *things are still the same. Dad and Mom still fight a lot. They both embarrass me, and I'm*
> *still invisible to both of them. They haven't learned how to be parents—I still have the job!*

Sandy is angry that her parents haven't changed much, even though her father is
now sober. For Sandy, getting better means changing other behaviors besides drinking. Both her parents are adult children of alcoholics and had no role models themselves for healthy parenting. In many ways, the problems that Sandy faces with them
have more to do with the way her parents were parented than the fact that her father
is an alcoholic.

Sandy's parents need to tune into Sandy's needs as an adolescent and her feelings as the child of an alcoholic. Children of alcoholics often feel unloved and
responsible for their parents' problems (Sher, 1997). They need to feel that they
are listened to and that their opinions count, that they are important to you, and
that you will be available to them when they need you.

This is a tall order, but it can be done. Studies show that families can recover from alcoholism in a relatively short time (Moos & Moos, 1984). One day at a time you can develop the trust and closeness you and your children need to create a whole and healthy family. The first step is to understand how your children see you and your recovery, to listen to your children with an open heart.

Is That All There Is? Life After Survival

When sobriety comes, children expect everything to become smooth and wonderful. They are not prepared for the long period of adjustment that Mom and Dad have to go through. They are not prepared for a worsening of the relationship between their parents, a common occurrence in newly recovering couples who may be honestly examining their commitment to one another for the first time in years.

One of the biggest disappointments children of alcoholics face is the realization that when the drinking stops, their lives don't immediately become the fantasy happy household that they imagined (Moos & Billings, 1982). Sophie, a 16-year-old daughter of an alcoholic, put it this way:

> I guess I thought that Mom would be like the mothers on TV when Dad got sober. Instead what I got was what I already had, but worse, because now I couldn't convince myself it could be different. I guess when I think about it, I must have imagined that some wicked witch put a curse on my family and when Dad got sober, the curse would be lifted. Mom would become a beautiful queen, Dad would be the handsome king, and I would be the indulged princess. But obviously, it hasn't worked out that way.

For the children of alcoholics who had ideas of becoming the perfect family, real life after sobriety can be a shock and a disappointment. The child may express this by becoming involved in alcohol abuse, truancy, or other delinquent behavior.

Loss: A Special Issue

One of the many losses children experience in recovery is the loss of the special role they may have played when their parent was actively drinking (Sher, 1997). Felicia, 13, talks about how she felt when her mother started taking over again:

> I felt very resentful. It used to be just Dad and me, and while I wanted Mom to be part of that, I really didn't have to worry about her butting in because she was drunk all the time or Dad was mad at her. Now I understand, but then I felt really betrayed by Dad when he started to let Mom order me around again. I mean, I used to make sure Dad had supper when he came home from work, not Mom, so why should she get my privileges now? It was very confusing for me. I wasn't used to having Mom as a mother. I was used to treating her like a younger sister and to treating Dad sort of like a husband sometimes and a father sometimes.

I know it was wrong, and Dad tells me it wasn't supposed to be that way and that we all need to go back to what we were supposed to be, but I miss being special to Dad. I also don't see where Mom gets the right to boss me around now. I mean, she tells me to be home by nine o'clock! I used to stay out until one in the morning whenever I wanted to. So long as I had breakfast ready and went to school and did my chores, Dad didn't care. I feel lost now, and angry, and guilty for feeling angry. I mean, I should be happy, so how come I'm not? Can you tell me why?

This issue of loss of a special place in the newly sober parent's life is very significant for children of alcoholics (Sher, 1997). Parents need to help their children adjust to new roles. Parents need to be sensitive to feelings of resentment previously unsupervised children might feel by appropriate parent concern. You will need to allow your child to go through the natural grieving process that accompanies loss. This may include a phase in which your child will try to bargain to retain some of his or her special privileges or tasks.

Felicia wasn't so sure she wanted her mother to make breakfast and take care of her father, especially if it meant that she would lose some of her well-earned freedoms in the process. Felicia's mother needs to be sensitive to the issue and gradually take back her role as mother. She needs to inform Felicia that while she is no longer needed to do the mother role in the house, she is still valued and respected. Felicia's mother will also have to examine what a reasonable curfew for Felicia is, given Felicia's past history in the family as a responsible family member.

There may also be a period of anger. Anger is a natural reaction to change and loss. You may be confused by your children's anger at a time when you feel they should be happy. You will need to remember that your recovery from alcoholism or its effects, while it may be something your children want, may still spark fear or resentment.

Eventually children will accept the changes in you, in their families, and in themselves, and they will learn to live within a healthy family, but it will take time!

Recovery Is Often Not About Kids

Children are often the forgotten people in the early stages of recovery from alcoholism. Often the first message they get from their parents and the treatment professional is that recovery will not include them.

As tears well up in her eyes, Sandy recalls her introduction to what recovery was going to be like for her and her younger brother Lance:

I couldn't believe it. The alcoholism counselor who was working with Dad called me and Lance into his office and told us that we needed to help Dad, now that he was trying to get sober. He told us Mom and Dad were going through a hard time and that we should try not to put any unnecessary stress on them. On them! Can you believe that? What did he think had been going on for the last 15 years? For as long as I can remember I have been trying to avoid putting stress on them. Who did he think was taking care of Mom every time she fell apart? Who did he think did the cooking, washing, Christmas shopping, and counseling for everyone? Who did he think helped raise Lance? And he had the nerve to tell Lance that he was supposed to help Dad and Mom now! Lance was 8 at the time and he was supposed to help Dad and Mom? I think all adults are crazy. When do we get taken care of? I was supposed to take care of them when he's sober? And you know what, I left the counselor's office feeling guilty for not wanting to help out anymore! Even thinking about that now I feel angry and like no one will ever see what I need ever ... ever ... ever.

Sandy's introduction to the helping professions is not unusual for children of alcoholics. Sandy was the highest functioning member of her family, and the therapist made a classic error. He was asking her to continue raising her parents, and he gave her the message that recovery was not going to be about the kids. Parents often fall into the trap of letting the child who has been Mother's little helper or Daddy's little girl continue in the role of Superkid after the drinking has stopped. This is particularly true of the sober spouse who has gotten used to having an extra set of hands around to do the shopping, cleaning, cooking, and banking. Sandy's parents were concerned because she was failing two of her subjects when they brought her into therapy. It took them a while to realize that Sandy was failing because she felt ignored by them and abused by all the adult work she was still being asked to do. Children often act out anger in behavior such as drunkenness, promiscuity, or poor school performance (Earls et al., 1998). This is a response to the message that the only way to get taken care of is to be dysfunctional. Children of alcoholics learn early in life that being responsible gets rewarded by more unwanted responsibility (Kumpfer & DeMarsh, 1986).

You can help your children by letting them know that recovery is a family process. Give them an age-appropriate role in the family, and help them to learn how to be children instead of little adults. Let them know that your family values each individual equally and that everyone, including the children, will share in the family's attention.

Move Beyond The Past; Help Your Children to Do The Same

At all times, but especially during the early recovery stages, it is important to begin to unburden your children from the baggage of the past. In the actively alcoholic family, the alcoholic is constantly focused on drinking, and the spouse or the adult child of the alcoholic is constantly focused on the alcoholic. When the alcoholic was actively addicted, everyone was concerned with parent's drinking. Once a parent gets sober, children expect that to change. They expect and really need their families to leave the alcoholism behind. Instead, what generally materializes in recovering alcoholic families is a demand for everyone to be concerned with a parent's sobriety. This is compounded by the fact that during the course of family treatment, the alcoholic and the sober spouse may discover that they are adult children of alcoholics. All this can be extremely disappointing to the child.

"I Don't Care If I'm At Risk!": Getting Distance from Addiction

Most of the time they still only think of themselves. All Dad ever talks about is alcoholism and staying straight, and it makes me nuts. It makes me want to go out and get high to get even. We still have to make them feel better. They still fight all the time, and now they get on my case more than before, because now they think they have to be superparents. Mom is constantly telling me I'm at risk to be an alcoholic like Dad and my grandfather and Uncle Jack. I mean, how does she know I'm going to be an alcoholic? Dad wants me to go to an AA meeting with him. I hate alcoholism. I don't want anything to do with it. I don't care if Mom is adult child of an alcoholic, all I want is a normal family. So what if my Dad doesn't drink or snort coke anymore? He still thinks he's God, and he treats me like a kid. I mean, who does he think did all his work all these years, the tooth fairy?

—Quentin, 14, the child of Brad, a recovering alcoholic and cocaine user in AA, and Lynette, who attends Al-Anon meetings

When a parent stops drinking, the last thing the children want to hear about is addiction. It is normal for traumatized children to want to distance themselves from the source of their trauma once the trauma is over. For children of alcoholics, this often takes the form of not wanting to talk about or hear about drinking or any recovery program the parents may be involved with, be it AA, NA, Al-Anon or ACoA. Children tend to view their parents' interest in these subjects as a continuation of the family's focus on alcoholism.

Most parents who have been affected by alcoholism fear that their children will become alcoholic. The statistics bear out this fear: children of alcoholics are four times more likely to become alcoholics than the general population (Kumpfer, 1999) and are more likely to marry an alcoholic (Nici, 1979; James & Goldman, 1971). This does not mean, however, that your child will become an alcoholic or drug addict. Your child is at risk for addiction. Accept that fact just like you accept the fact that your child is at risk for many other diseases that may run in your family, like heart disease or diabetes. You need to educate your children so they can understand what may happen in the future, and then you need to let go. If you project negatively about your children's future, you will create an atmosphere of fear and anxiety in your household, which is not good for you or your children. The least effective way to influence your children is by moralizing and smothering them with concern. Let your children know they are at risk when drinking becomes an option for them for them, but do it in an unemotional way, stating facts rather than feelings.

"Help! My Parents Are Freaking Out!": Understanding the Program

Children need help to understand your 12-step program. Many children whose parents are in "the program" think their parents have entered a strange cult.

Sandy explains what life was like after the treatment center when Dad and Mom joined 12-step programs:

> It was like they had totally freaked out. My Dad and Mom started talking about the 12-steps of AA and God and a bunch of weird stuff like that. I could never get a straight answer from them. If I asked a question about some problem, they would quote some AA or Al-Anon slogan or "step" to me; it was like their brains were controlled by AA and they couldn't think for themselves. And my father was always talking about Bill Wilson (the founder of AA) and the program of Alcoholics Anonymous. The "program"—it sounded like they were Moonies or something. I didn't recognize these people at all. At least before I knew what to expect from them. Now it was like they were strangers.
>
> I mean, talk about weird! My Dad never believed in God, and he never went to church. All of a sudden he was talking about his higher power, meaning God, all the time. He made us all say the serenity prayer before dinner. Mom constantly had all these weird women around talking about stuff I didn't understand. I would listen to them sometimes, and all they would talk about was how to live with an alcoholic, like nothing else existed. Sometimes I would see someone crying and talking about how she was the adult child of an alcoholic. Then my mother would get all choked up and look at me like I was going to die or something. It scared me to see those adults freaking out.
>
> I thought when Dad stopped drinking, I wouldn't have to hear about alcoholism ever again, and now that's all they ever talk about. In a way it's worse than ever before. Before we never talked about it, and we needed to, because Dad had a problem. Now he always talks about his alcoholism, and Mom's also talking about how her father's drinking affected her. I didn't even know he was an alcoholic. I just wish for once we could be a normal family and not be sooo heavy!

Most children are ambivalent about their parents' entry into 12-step programs. Children are usually not informed about the nature of AA and Al-Anon and are very confused about what goes on in these programs. Since it is natural for them to not want to talk about alcoholism and to put the bad memories of the drinking days behind them, they are confused by their parents' constant focus on the disease. They feel resentful because meetings now take both parents away from them, and they see this as unfair. They thought that once their parent got sober, they would all be together. Instead, they find there will be less time together, not more, and on top of that, the sober spouse is now abandoning them as well.

"I Might as Well Become One, Too": Feeling Replaced

One reaction that children have to AA and Al-Anon, which may be conscious or unconscious, is to feel that they will be left out of the family unless they become an alcoholic or marry one. Listen to what Sophie, 16, has to say about her parents:

> It's like the only thing they care about is the people in AA and Al-Anon. I brought home my report card last week and had straight As. I went into the living room to show Dad and he was talking to Mom about this teenager he met in AA who was sober and had been strung out on cocaine. He was saying how much courage it took for this kid and how much he respected him. He said the kid asked him to be his sponsor and Dad said he would. He said that he was going to take him to a meeting next Friday...he didn't even remember that Friday night was my induction into my school honor society. And Mom's no different. All she ever talks about are these young girls who have real struggles with their husbands and that I shouldn't complain about my life! I mean, I guess you don't count in my family unless you're a drunk or married to one. Dad never has any time for us, but he has time for a drug addict. I guess I should become a drug addict and ask him to be my sponsor; maybe then he'd pay attention to me.

Sophie's parents were totally unaware of their daughter's feelings. They did not know that she felt undervalued by them. They were not aware of the messages they were unwittingly sending to her about their priorities. Certainly, Sophie's father had no idea how replaced his daughter felt by his decision to sponsor a young person. Parents in 12-step programs need to be tuned in to these subtle, powerful reactions.

The remedy is to take the time to find out how your children feel about your activity in AA, NA, Al-Anon, or ACoA meetings. You need to become sensitive to the feelings of jealousy and competition that your new relationships might engender in your children. This does not mean that your participation in self-help programs is bad for your children. It mans that you must respect their reactions and reassure them that they, your children, are important to you. It means you need to be careful about the extent to which you impose the philosophy of the self-help programs on your children.

What children need most is to see parents who are changing their behaviors to create better communication and greater acceptance of individual differences in the family system. What they need least is to be introduced to an alien set of values and an alien jargon at a very confusing point in their lives. Your enthusiasm for AA and Al-Anon would be best expressed by working the principles of the 12-step programs to create a positive, loving environment in your home. This is true family recovery.

Dealing with Stress in the Family

The most destructive element in an alcoholic family is chronic stress. Stress can cause physical diseases in children such as peptic ulcers, bronchial asthma, high blood pressure, migraine headaches, and backaches. It is often asserted that adult children of alcoholics may be suffering from a variety of posttraumatic stress disorders (Earls et al., 1998) similar to those noted in returning combat veterans, which is induced by the chronic stress suffered in childhood from living in an alcoholic family system. For some, home is like a war. Stress in an alcoholic home can stem from the controlling behavior of the adult child of an alcoholic or the chronically inconsistent behavior of an alcoholic parent. It is aggravated by the twin fears of violence and the fear that the family will be separated. If incest and child abuse are involved, the stresses are magnified a hundredfold.

The changes and uncertainty that come when a parent recovers from alcoholism heighten (at least for a while) the stress that your children have to deal with. It is important to help your children develop positive coping strategies to handle the stress in their lives. From their pint of view many of the aspects of recovery that you count as pluses, they score as minuses (Dies & Burghardt, 1991). The new friends, recovery programs, and growth that will work for you will not answer your children's problems.

You will need to help your children develop support systems outside the family and inside it (Natasi & DeZolt, 1994). Outside sources of support for your children can include Student Assistance Programs, offered by many schools; Alateen or other groups for children of alcoholics, if your children are willing to go; or any youth group activity that allows children to share feelings—the Scouts, 4-H, Big Brother/Sisters, or faith-based youth groups are some examples.

Creating a similar support system within your family will compensate for the lack of organization that previously existed within the family. Organizing family support meetings each week can help. This will structure family discussions and lead to greater feelings of safety.

How do you do this? With your children,

- *Specify a time for a weekly meeting.* For example, Sunday afternoon after lunch.

- *Agree on how long the meeting with be.* For example, no longer than half an hour, or one hour.

- *Develop an agenda.* For example, everyone write down their week's activities and what they need to accomplish them: transportation, a later dinner than usual, and so on.

· *Begin the meeting with each person saying something positive or funny.* This
can go a long way in developing the resilience of your family members and to
having the meetings looked forward to as a fun events.

Although anger is a normal emotional response to stress and loss, in general,
children tend to feel guilty if they show anger (Youngs, 1985). Give your children
the message that it is okay to express anger, to help them learn how to express and
communicate what they feel. This will be difficult if you are learning this skill for
yourself at the same time. Just remember, no one grows up having all these skills,
and all parents, even those without alcoholism in their families, have problems
expressing feeling and communicating with their children. You are certainly not
alone.

Summary

When parents enter recovery, there is still much work that needs to occur within
the family, particularly with the children. Children need help in negotiating their
parents' recovery. Many things about their parents' recovery may be confusing to
children. The self-help programs need to be explained with care and in an age-
appropriate manner, and you need to ensure that the child is not lost in the confusion of entering treatment and recovery programs. Remember, loss is a special
issue for children from alcoholic families. They may act out anger or other feelings
as a response to the loss of special roles they had in the family. They will react to
other changes in the family system, as well. Being available to your children and
sensitive to their needs and feelings will make their transition into recovery con-
siderably easier.

You can break the cycle of dysfunctional parenting. It takes a commitment to
listen to your children with your heart and with your head. To succeed you will
need to take a compassionate view of the impact your recovery has on your children, and to suspend your own ideas about your children and what they need. To
become a good parent you must become teachable, and allow your children to be
one source of your education.

This means learning to listen to your children in a special way. Children often
speak in codes that need to be deciphered. Learning to read your child's code and
understand his or her feelings will increase the intimacy between you. Letting your
child know that he or she has been truly heard and responded to will increase self-
esteem in your child and create new possibilities for health and happiness.

CHAPTER 5

For Parents and Caregivers Who Are Adult Children of Addicts

Sometimes I am simply overwhelmed. My father was an alcoholic, my mother was the child of an alcoholic, both my grandmothers were adult children of alcoholics, and my husband is a recovering alcoholic. I go to Al-Anon and Adult Children of Alcoholics meetings, my husband goes to AA. My kids think my husband and I have gone crazy, and I worry what Rick's drinking did to our kids, Lisa and Julien. I also worry about the effect I had on them. All I ever do is worry and watch and wait for them to show the signs of alcoholism; it's like waiting for a bomb to drop. This cannot be the way it was meant to be. There must be another way. I'm just as upset now as I was before, and I don't know how to be any other way.

—Claudia, age 34, parent

So What's Normal, and Where Do I Begin?

Like many adult children of alcoholics, Claudia is in a cycle of fear and despair. She has no guidelines for parenting. Her childhood was one of chaos, confusion, inconsistency, and abuse. Because their own upbringing has been so crazy and confusing, many parents who are adult children of addicts have no barometer by which to gauge their own parenting; they are obliged to parent in the dark.

All Claudia knows how to do is wait and watch, which is what her mother did. To be a healthy parent, Claudia needs to find out what family life is like outside her own alcoholic family and what healthy parenting looks like. She also needs to understand there is no such thing as a "normal" home.

The Impact of Addiction

Letting Go of Perfection

Adult children of alcoholics (and other addicts) often think that "normal" means "perfect," and that somewhere in the world perfect families exist. But perfectionism is a double-edged sword that can cause one to become immobilized and give up, or become an excuse to do nothing, for perfectionism can never be reached. It can also be a reason to push oneself relentlessly to achieve high goals, all in an attempt to prove one's worth. Either reaction to perfectionism is a response to the pain of rejection from childhood, and children of addicts are susceptible to both of these "perfection traps" at any age.

No one does well when judged against perfection. The fantasy that other families are normal and perfect leaves adult children of alcoholics like Claudia fearful and alone, wondering how to begin to be a healthy parent. The first step in becoming a healthy parent is to discard the notion of perfection, and allow yourself to become teachable and vulnerable as a person who happens to be a parent or caregiver.

The second step to healthy parenting for adult children of alcoholics is to face the effect that growing up in an alcoholic home has had on your own parenting. This is not easy. You may find that you are continuing with your children where your parents left off with you. Having had an alcoholic parent directly impacts the way that you parent. Many adult children of alcoholics have an overwhelming emphasis on issues of interpersonal safety, including long-standing serious problems with trust, guardedness, hypervigilance, a need for control and the fear of loss of control, cognitive and affective denial, all-or-nothing thinking, and an overriding, inappropriate assumption of responsibility for others.

This has many implications for ACoA parents. Some may overreact to changes they cannot control, and tend to be either super-responsible or extremely irresponsible. Seeing the world as black or white does not leave room for compromise.

Many adult children of alcoholics are terrified of abandonment and will do anything to hold onto a relationship. Any or all of these characteristics will interfere with healthy parenting at times. It is no wonder that adult children of alcoholics often feel lost and frightened when they become parents.

If you grew up in an alcoholic home, you probably did not get the nurturing or support you needed as a child, and you may still long for that now. Sometimes adult children of alcoholics feel embittered by their childhood deprivation and will resent the nurturing they give their children, especially if the children don't appear grateful for the attention. Of course, children generally aren't grateful for the attention they receive. They feel that attention is their right, and it is. Adults raised in an alcoholic home will often not understand this because no one paid attention to them growing up, or the attention they received was inappropriate.

These are some of the negative effects that growing up in an alcoholic home has on your parenting. But believe it or not, growing up in an alcoholic home can also have some *positive* effects.

Resilience

Resilience is the ability to bounce back from adversity. It is the ability to learn from hardships that life offers and use this to grow and develop inner resources that are helpful when life next challenges us (O'Gorman, 1994).

Adult children of alcoholics are resilient people. Quite frankly, they have had to be to survive what is usually a very difficult set of life circumstances. But many ACoAs do not merely survive, they learn to thrive in the face of these obstacles, developing key parts of themselves. For example, many ACoAs have a great capacity for nurturing and a willingness to help others; often they are excellent at reading other people's emotions and intentions. Because they are so sensitive to their environments, ACoAs are more attuned to the people around than most of the general population. This may be why so many ACoAs choose careers in the "helping professions." And many adult children of alcoholics show tremendous courage and a will to forge ahead in the face of incredible adversity. They learned how to take risks as children, and as adults they have learned to successfully channel this into productive means. Among their number are great world leaders, past and present.

As you learn to be a healthy parent, you will need to use these and other assets you have to enhance your skills while you work on dealing with your deficits. And you can teach yourself to notice your own resilience, as well. Try the following:

- *Develop a vocabulary that describes your strengths.* Remember, most of the time you have focused on what needs to be done and not on what you have accomplished, so focus on your accomplishments and see what strengths are found here. For example, are you colorful? Funny? Thoughtful? A good cook? Someone with a sharp wit or a quick tongue?

- *Ask those close to you to point out when you are using your resilience.* Instead of asking the important people in your life to help you find your faults, ask them to let you know when you are doing it right.

- *Become aware of situations where you need to be strong*—where your resilience could be helpful to you—and begin to see yourself being successful here.

- *Consciously decide how to use your resilience when you are in these situations. Imagine different ways of handling old situations, such as dealing with your children when they are yelling at each other.*

- *Think about how you want to be seen in this situation.* Think about how you *prefer* to act, and experiment with some new resilience behaviors. (O'Gorman, 2004).

As you think about your resilience, you will also need to consider what stimulated you to grow in these ways and to develop the strengths that you have. You will need to assess the specific ways that growing up in your alcoholic home affected you and face what that means to the way you interact with your children.

No one can parent without dealing with the way they were parented. You cannot give love and support to your children without tapping into your own experience of love and support. For adult children of alcoholics, this can be very painful. It will take courage and commitment to make meaningful changes in your parenting. To make real change, creating a new cycle of hope and love in your children, you will have to challenge a basic fear of failure. Take the risk: begin to think of yourself as resilient!

Common Parenting Styles of ACoAs
The Hypervigilant Parent

> *I can't stand it anymore! My mother just won't stop worrying about me. I'm 15 years old and she treats me like I'm a baby. She is constantly hovering over me. It's like I'm under a microscope all the time. She is always looking for problems. It's like I'm not supposed to have problems, and if I do, she's supposed to solve them. She's always telling me what's good for me. When I complain, she tells me that she never had involved parents and I should be grateful that she cares about what's happening in my life. I wouldn't mind if I felt she just wanted to help, but it feels more like she wants to live my life for me, or with me. She's always complaining how she was robbed of her childhood because she had to grow up so fast because her father was an alcoholic. Well, she's not letting me have my childhood because she won't let me grow up!*
>
> —Lisa, age 15

RULE: *Children need guidance, not control.*

Adult children of alcoholics are hypervigilant. They constantly scan their environment for possible danger, a coping mechanism learned as child. This hypervigilance makes ACoAs extremely sensitive to their environment. They are exceptionally good at reading the slightest change in mood or situation based on all kinds of observational skills that the general population doesn't use. Obviously if you are a young child in an alcoholic home, this acute awareness is very useful skill.

But hypervigilance can become a problem for the ACoA parent. Children need to develop self-reliance. The infant needs to learn that all her needs will not always be met; the toddler needs to learn many things through trial and error. They hypervigilant parent interferes with this learning process by reading the child's needs and immediately responding to them. In some cases, the response may not be necessary or helpful for the child. Younger children never learn to accept disappointment if all their needs are always met. They grow up with an unrealistic sense that their needs should and will be met whenever they express them.

Another outcome of this type of parenting is the feeling of being smothered that Lisa talked about, or a feeling that you are defective in some way because you must be watched all the time.

The Anxious Parent

Many adult children of alcoholics suffer from chronic anxiety. As a result of the trauma faced in childhood, they are subject to nameless fears and project these fears onto their family members, their children in particular. This is why children of ACoAs often describe their families as having many of the same fears, anxieties, and behaviors as in an alcoholic family.

As Claudia said:

I just didn't realize the impact my worrying had on my children. I didn't realize that the way I was expressing concern was undermining Lisa's self-confidence. I've grown up being anxious, waiting for the other shoe to drop, and it usually did! My mother would wake me up at night to wait with her until my father got home when he was out on a drunk. She would sit in the kitchen with me making small talk while she wrung her hands. Every few minutes she would get up to check to see that my younger brothers were okay and then keep asking me if I was all right. I used to hate that about her.

There were always problems with money when I was a child, and my mother was always fearful that we wouldn't have enough to eat. Her worrying made her old before her time. It was very sad. Even now as I think back, I feel how sad it was that she spent most of her time waiting and worrying and very little of her life living. I remember promising myself that I would never live like that, but I guess I've not been as successful as I thought. My husband makes enough money and has been sober a long time now, but I still worry. Old habits die hard.

I never realized the baggage from the past that I was putting on my kids. I was walking around as though I was still living with my alcoholic father. I hovered around Lisa like a hawk, just like I used to hover around my younger sister. But then it was necessary. I never knew what my mother or father would do, or who would be visiting, my father's drunken

friends or my mother's. I forget that the children have a safe home and that Rick and I can
continue to provide that for all our children.

Anxious parents create anxious children. An anxious home is one in which fear dominates. Children need a secure environment in which to thrive. Adult children of alcoholics need to learn how to feel safe so they can communicate that message to their children. It can be done. The ACoA parent needs to learn to separate the past from the present. It is very hard for adult children to admit they are finally safe and that they no longer need to be afraid as they were as children.

Jealousy: A Special Issue

Our children remind us of the wondrous, open, and vulnerable world that children inhabit. They help us remember to keep in touch with those aspects of ourselves. For adult children of alcoholics, special issues are raised when you try to connect with the child within.

Claudia says angrily:

> *I was taught to deny my emotional reality, so it is difficult for me to know what I really feel, much less what my children are feeling. I don't know what I am supposed to feel in any situation, so I pretend I don't feel anything or fake what I think might be an appropriate feeling. I'm either a whirlwind of emotion or I feel nothing. I know what I've learned to value my brain above my heart. Sometimes my contradictory feelings are confusing. When I'm with the children and really close, I sometimes feel jealous of them for having me as a parent. Isn't that strange?*

Jealousy of one's children is a special issue for adult children of alcoholics. It is hard for many ACoAs to accept the reality of their childhoods. As an ACoA you may be faced with the strange and uncomfortable feeling of resenting yourself for being a loving parent. This is very difficult to deal with. Like Claudia, many ACoA parents are caught in a web of fear and confusion when faced simultaneously with the contradictory feelings of love and resentment.

As an ACoA, you must learn to separate the feelings you have toward your children from those you have toward your parents. The resentment that may rise up is aimed at your parents, but you unconsciously deflect it toward your children. As you build a secure and nurturing home for your children, the child in you will rage at the recognition of the deprivation he or she suffered. It is important that you understand that the child in you wants to get even when it is faced with pain. It may want to punish your children for its deprivation, rather than allow you to nurture your children.

This does not mean that you shouldn't feel. You need to feel your sadness for the sake of yourself as well as your children. You will have to parent the child in you and your children with the same understanding and love. You will need to make sure you do not act out your anger against your children that is really meant for your parents. In time your anger will resolve itself and you will move to other stages of recovery. Meanwhile, you will need to learn to live with contradictory feelings and keep nurturing your children in spite of the rage it may make you feel.

Claudia is typical of many ACoAs who, as adults, had to learn for the first time to deal with feelings locked away since childhood, but who also have to be parents and help their children have healthy and full emotional lives. Claudia needs to learn that one can have mutually contradictory feelings at the same time. She needs to have her feelings and not to minimize or dismiss them.

Denial of feelings is a chief characteristic of the alcoholic family. It is the breeding ground for denial of alcoholism in the adult. Alcohol does not have to be present to have an alcoholic family system; a system that breeds denial of emotion can be called an alcoholic family.

> **RULE:** *Encourage your children to express their feelings, and validate their feelings.*

Working on Yourself Is the Beginning

The task of the ACoA parent is to break the cycle of denial. Without work on oneself, the family pattern of denial and minimizing of feelings continues and is passed on from generation to generation. Claudia is attempting to break the cycle, and so is Mary. Mary explains how she got help.

> *I was lost at first, I didn't know where to begin. A friend of mine had read a book about adult children of alcoholics and gave it to me. I was flabbergasted. I was happy, confused, angry, and sad all at the same time. In short, I was a mess. Fred couldn't help. He was too busy trying to get his AA program straight. I found a self-help group for adult children of alcoholics and things immediately got better. I found support and validation in those rooms. For the first time, I was told that I was important, that I mattered and that I had a right to feel and express my feelings. For the first time I was told that my parents were the sick ones, not me. I had to admit I didn't know basic stuff about myself, so I also entered therapy to help sort out my childhood and find the missing pieces so I could parent my kids.*

Learning to Give up Control

Like Mary, you may need to learn how to play with your children.

> *I feel so uptight when I take Andy and his friends to the playground. I really never learned how to relax as a child. In my family you stayed ever-vigilant just in case Dad or Mom had a problem. My father was always drunk, and my mother was always sick or upset, so*

who could have fun? Now when my 8-year-old wants to play, I don't know how. Actually, it's very painful for me to watch to other parents laughing and being silly with their kids when there I am unable to let go and wanting to so badly. I just have trouble being spontaneous.

It's also a problem for Fred. I remember the last time we all went out for a picnic together. It was a mess. Fred and I had planned the day so thoroughly there was no time to have fun. We ended up dragging the kids from fun place to fun place and never staying long enough anywhere to enjoy ourselves. I know now the reason Fred and I were afraid of staying in one place is because we don't know how to just have fun and were unwilling to admit it and let our kids show us how.

Mary is not alone. Many adult children of alcoholics have problems learning how to relax and have fun. ACoA parents may view a family outing as a checklist of tasks to be completed. The overachieving ACoA will often over-program family activities, trying to create the perfect event. For adult children of alcoholics, going with the flow and letting things just happen is frightening. Breaking the old pattern of compulsive self-control feels wrong and self-indulgent. Many adult children report that when they are spontaneous and let go of some of their control, they feel as though they are drunk; they feel that they are doing something wrong, something potentially dangerous. Their only role model for "letting go" has usually been a drunken parent; thus the association between being spontaneous and being drunk (misbehaving or out of control) is very strong.

For the adult child of the alcoholic to be able to become a free and spontaneous parent, he or she will have to face the belief that being spontaneous is not like being drunk and therefore bad. But control is like a drug for adult children of alcoholics. They are often accustomed to managing everyone and everything around them. This need to control one's environment is learned behavior for ACoAs. If you grew up in a home where you had no control over your environment, you may have learned to value control above all else because it is what you needed more than anything else. The child of the alcoholic wants to control his parents because they won't control themselves. The child of the alcoholic often grows up watching adults constantly lose control and learns to hate any situation where people do not control themselves. This growth pattern has a direct impact on the adult child's ability to let go and have fun.

Mary and Fred will need to work on helping each other let go. This will often happen first in simply learning how to play in small ways. Maybe Fred and Mary will go out alone with no advance planning. It could mean taking one Friday night together and seeing where the spirit moves them to go. This can be like going on an adventure if it is done with the proper attitude and not seen as a prescription for dysfunctional behavior.

RULE: *Let your children help you remember how to play.*

Take time out to play hopscotch or jacks or have a tea party with your kids. You'll be surprised to find that the child inside you has been waiting for a chance to get out. The rewards for letting your inner child out will be manifold and will provide fun dividends in many areas of your life. Planning less and being more emotionally available to your children will increase your ability to really play with your kids and experience joy in your life.

Seeing Beyond the Extremes

RULE: *Life is not black and white.*

Adult children of alcoholics need to learn to accept the fact that most situations are gray areas. As stated earlier, ACoAs tend to see the world either black or white, which is one outcome of growing up in an alcoholic home. Mary talks about growing up in her alcoholic home and how she learned to think only in terms of extremes:

> There were no gray areas in our home. My father would fluctuate between telling me I was his special, wonderful little girl or telling me I was no good. The same was true of my mother. I would come home from school and, depending on her mood or how my father had acted that day, she would be either screaming at me that I was nothing but a lazy good-for-nothing brat or praising me for being her smart little helper. I learned to expect extremes as a way of life. It's all I know. So of course it's hard for me to break the habit of seeing everything in extremes with my own kids. The sad part is I hated it when my parents pulled that all-good or all-bad stuff. It was frustrating and made me feel crazy. And then I catch myself doing the same thing with my kids.

Confusion about your own feelings makes it difficult for you to bring emotional clarity to your children. It is much easier to live in a world of black and white. To see the gray areas in the world means allowing yourself to feel more anxiety. It means realizing there are no bad answers. It means having to sort things out instead of jumping to conclusions. Most of all, it means accepting that you are not all bad or good and that your parents were not all bad or good.

Changing Direction
Feedback

Checking with healthy friends and getting feedback is especially important for adult children of alcoholic parents. You need to bounce your perceptions of your family members off other people in order to really see how your perceptions may have been colored by your childhood experience of living in an alcoholic home. If you view this process of getting feedback as a learning process, it can be fun. It will help you to see the patterns of perceptions you have about yourself, your partner, and your children. If you recognize that many of the attitudes you have are tempered by your childhood, you will be able to change direction and create healthy role models for your children. Getting feedback will help you to see that intimacy is not necessarily smothering, that being spontaneous is not the same as being irrational, and that letting down and being relaxed will not bring on depression. Getting feedback will help you to see your children in a more objective light.

It takes time to change old habits. All-or-nothing thinking will not go away overnight, and you cannot wish it away. It is a learned behavior that will take time to unlearn. Adult children of alcoholics tend to be hypercritical of themselves—an unfortunate quality that makes them frustrated and may cause them to give up trying to change. If you approach your behaviors that change as habits that take time to adjust, you will experience a higher degree of success. Behavioral change is a daily struggle, and you will need patience and perseverance to be successful.

Setting Limits

Children need to have clear limits and need to understand what is acceptable and unacceptable behavior. Adult children of alcoholics have a difficult time with limit setting. Often either no limits were set for them as children or limits were arbitrary and imposed with violence. In either case, there was no positive role modeling for self-discipline. Adult children of alcoholics have grown up in a world where the unacceptable was commonplace. If Dad wanted to fall asleep in the garage, he did. If Mom was beaten by Dad on Friday night, it was okay to pretend it never happened on Saturday morning. In fact, hitting, cursing, and acts of humiliation are acceptable in many alcoholic homes. Adult children of alcoholics grow up without knowing what is appropriate behavior.

A basic task of parents is to teach their children guidelines for operating in the world in an appropriate manner. This means learning what acceptable and unacceptable behavior is and accepting limits on oneself in order to model them for your children. Needless to say, ACoAs have problems teaching these skills to their children when they still have to learn them for themselves. Says Claudia,

> I remember a fight Rick and I had a few years ago, in which we were screaming at one another and got violent. He hit me and I hit him back, and we were shouting profanities at one another, just the way my parents had done almost every day of my life. I had become immune to that kind of behavior and thought nothing of fighting that way. Lisa was about 8 at the time. I went into the kitchen to make a cup of coffee and found her under the kitchen table crying. I realized I was terrorizing her the way I had been terrorized. I

realized then that hitting and screaming could no longer be acceptable behavior for me,
regardless of the way Rick behaved. It shook me up to see her so frightened. It brought
back all my childhood fears when my own parents fought and how I would pray that they
wouldn't kill one another. I realized if Rick and I continued to fight that way Lisa and
Julien would learn to do the same thing, and I swore then that I would break this cycle of
hate and violence or die trying. From that point on I examined my behavior as a wife and
parent from a role-modeling point of view. Eventually Rick also saw what we were doing
to ourselves and the kids by making that type of behavior acceptable.

Not all of us get shocked into self-examination the way Claudia did. Claudia
understands that as an adult child of an alcoholic, she needs to examine her actions
to see if she is modeling acceptable or unacceptable behavior. She understands that
unless she sets appropriate limits on herself, her children will never accept her
setting limits on them. She took responsibility for her parenting by beginning to
screen her own and her husband's behavior.

Spontaneous Age Regression

As they begin to deal with the past, adult children of alcoholics come in touch with many
overwhelming and painful memories and emotions. For many, these feelings surface
when they enter a 12-step recovery program. Here, often for the first time, they share
memories of a childhood that they have repressed for many years. That can be disori-
enting. Many adult children of alcoholics report feeling like emotional volcanoes that
may erupt at any time. Indeed, an explosion of feelings often surges up during the first
years of recovery.

As an ACoA, once you begin to come to terms with your past, powerful feelings
can be provoked, and you may experience something called spontaneous age regression. This is a state in which a reminder from childhood, like a particular piece
of music or special phrase someone uses that reminds you of your parents, throws
you back into memories from the past, and so you begin responding as though you
were a child again (Gravitz & Bowden, 1985).

For all these reasons, early recovery is a very difficult time for adult children of
alcoholics. In an attempt to explain what is happening to their children or as a way
of attempting to find nurturance, ACoAs may reach out in inappropriate ways to
their children. They may start to lean on their children for emotional support in
ways that breed anger and resentment.

Lisa talks about her mother:

She tells me she is going through a tough time because she is having a lot of feelings about
her parents. She told me about how my grandfather beat her and sometimes touched her in
the wrong way. I mean, wow—that totally blew me away! She said she's not sure she's ever

felt loved. She even told me once that being the adult child of an alcoholic has affected her sex life, that she was promiscuous when she was younger, and now she's afraid of sex. Then she asked me if I ever felt that way. Can you believe that? I was totally embarrassed! My brother Julien found her in her room crying. She was holding a picture of her mother. He came to me totally freaked out. I wonder if she is losing it completely. I'm frightened for my brother. He gets upset when Mom starts crying or throwing things. I don't need Alateen; I need to go to a group for children of recovering adult children of alcoholics.

Lisa resents her mother needing her support. She wants her mother to be there for her. She needs her mother to be a parent. Claudia, on the other hand, is going through a very powerful time in her life and needs to experience what she is feeling. These situations are not mutually exclusive. Claudia needs to lean more on her husband her friends and less on her children.

Children are not small adults. They do not need to be sheltered entirely from their parents' emotions, but those emotions should be shared appropriately. Claudia's children are frightened for her and for themselves. Children need a safe and secure environment. When a parent seems emotionally unstable or does things that seem strange, children become insecure and worry about their parents. This creates the same type of stress and tension that exists in actively alcoholic homes.

RULE: *Reliving trauma is not necessarily healthy.*

Claudia is reliving a traumatic part of her past. She needs to learn how to deal with that experience in a healthy way. Many adult children of alcoholics think that more feeling is necessarily better and that if they keep reliving the traumatic experiences from their childhood, they will somehow exorcise their feelings about them. This is not so. Reliving trauma may turn into recreating trauma, which is harmful and unproductive for adult children of alcoholics or for those around them. In fact, staying stuck in the past does not allow the ACoA to make the necessary changes in the present.

RULE: *Share information appropriately.*

Sharing your childhood traumas carelessly with your children can traumatize them. Lisa was very upset with the information her mother gave her about her grandparents. Claudia needs to examine her motives for sharing that information. If her intention wasn't aimed at helping Lisa, then she shouldn't have shared it with her daughter. If it was aimed at getting even with her parents, then she has only succeeded in breeding another generation of resentment in her children.

You must exercise caution and discretion when sharing your childhood with your children. This is especially true when sharing your negative feelings toward their grandparents. Your children should not be put in the position where they must choose between you and their grandparents. This puts your children in the position of choosing between people they love. It is a no-win situation for the children and puts them under unnecessary stress.

Guidelines For Recovery

As an adult child from an alcoholic family, you are a survivor with many strengths. You need to identify with these strengths and work on the weaknesses. All too often, we hear ACoAs refer to themselves as "dysfunctional" because they have identified some negative coping patterns in themselves or recognized an area of life in which they feel blocked. This does not make one a dysfunctional person. What it points out is that adult children of alcoholics, like other people who have come from troubled families, need to examine and change some dysfunctional attitudes, beliefs, and behaviors.

Adult children of alcoholics tend to describe themselves in negative terms such as "sick" or "controlling." Who wants a sick parent, and what useful purpose is served by describing yourself that way? Does it enhance self-esteem to call oneself dysfunctional? This approach may only serve to increase your children's anxiety and confusion and increase their sense of insecurity. Children believe their parents. If you tell your young children you are sick, they will believe you. If you tell them alcoholism is a family disease, they will believe that, too. They will not understand it, but they will get the important part of the message, which is that there is something wrong with them. Children need their parents to help create supportive home environments that give them messages that they are all right. This is especially true for children who have lived with active alcoholism. Calling yourself and your family sick only confuses your children. Instead, work to understand your character traits and change them so that your family sees the product of your 12-step program in you.

Summary

The important thing to remember, as a recovering adult child of an alcoholic who is a parent or a foster parent, is that you only need to do the best you can in one day. There is no such thing as a perfect parent, just as there are no perfect children. As an ACoA, you will need to accept that there are certain weaknesses you may have as a parent. But you also have many strengths that you can pass on to your children. You will need to exercise caution in sharing the details of your childhood with your children and in sharing the traumatic feelings you may be reliving.

Recovery is a journey, by turns exciting, disturbing, overwhelming, enlightening, and eventually liberating. The promise of recovery comes from the example of those in the 12-step programs who have learned to live full and loving lives free from addiction and destructive dependencies. The best example of your recovery for your family is to be a consistent parent who can supply a loving and secure environment for his children. Life is a learning process for both parent and child. For adult children of alcoholics, there is a great deal to learn, but if you let yourself find joy in the journey, your life and your children's lives will be enriched immeasurably, and each of you can become all you were meant to be!

PART II

Parenting Through Addiction and Recovery

CHAPTER 6

A
12-Step Approach
to Parenting

I remember when my father died. There was so much inside I couldn't express. I was lost in a sea of feeling. I really loved him deeply, even though until the day he died our life together was full of disappointment. At the end we got somewhat closer, but we never made it past our fear of one another. I still wonder if he really loved me. I don't want my kids to grow up with those questions.

I love my kids. If anything were to happen to them, I don't know what I would do. I am doing everything I can to see to it that my kids feel my love. I want to make sure that we do reach past our fear, and that as their father, I teach them a new way. I want to give them a start in life I never had.

—Marvin, an adult child of a drug addict; also a recovering
drug addict and father to Jamel, Rasheem, and Quintara

This chapter is about *showing your love*, sharing your love, and paying the price that loving costs. No relationship you will ever have will be as intense as the relationship and bond you will have with your children. For all of us, but especially for people affected by addiction, childhood was a time of bittersweet memories and unanswered questions. Like Marvin, many adults raised in homes with addicts grew up not knowing whether their parents loved them. They grew up not knowing how to show love, unable to trust that love can exist without strings.

For many people affected by addiction, their first experience of receiving love and concern with no strings attached is in a 12-step program. Often, for people recovering from an addiction, the 12-step programs come to represent the first healthy family they've ever had.

> *Most people can't understand why I say I'm a grateful drug addict. They don't understand that Alcoholics Anonymous has given me a way of life more productive and satisfying than anything I experienced before. Before I came into AA, I was lost. AA has given me a whole new way to look at the world. I have learned the value of honesty, compassion, and fellowship. I have learned how to give and receive. Wilma feels the same way about Al-Anon.*
>
> *One of the biggest bonuses of being in our 12-step programs is the effect they have had on our family. When we apply the principles of the program to our parenting, it works wonders.*
>
> —Joseph, recovering drug addict; husband of Wilma;
> and father of Vernon, 10, and Akisha, 15

The 12-Step Program and Parenting

Alcoholics Anonymous has helped millions of alcoholics and drug addicts to get straight and stay straight. Its simple guidelines for living have inspired a plethora of self-help programs like Al-Anon, Overeaters Anonymous, Gamblers Anonymous, Narcotics Anonymous and Shoppers Anonymous, to name a few. All of these self-help programs are based on the 12 steps of AA.

Founded on the experience of the first hundred people who got sober in Alcoholics Anonymous, the 12 steps offer a combination of psychology, spirituality, and good old common sense. As Joseph pointed out, the 12 steps of AA can also help you be a better parent and enrich the quality of your family's home life. You can learn to share your love and to parent in a nurturing manner by applying the 12 steps.

The 12 Steps of AA: A Reinterpretation for Parenting

STEP 1: *We admitted we were powerless over alcohol— that our lives had become unmanageable.*

Admit powerlessness over your ability to protect your children from pain. Become willing to surrender to your love and not your control.

The first step in recovery programs calls for a willingness to admit powerlessness and unmanageability. This admission lays the groundwork for all the following steps in AA. This admission of powerlessness is also important for parents.

Parenting is a continual struggle between fear and love. The parent loves the child deeply and fears that harm will come to the child. This fear that one loved so much might be harmed overwhelms the parent, and so parents begin to believe that they can protect the child from harm (and thereby control their fear) by controlling the child. This is, of course, as futile as a drug addict trying to control his drinking or a spouse trying to control a drug addict. It simply is not possible.

The attempt to manage one's fear for one's child through control is often destructive to the relationship between parent and child. It breeds rebellion and anger in the child and bitterness in the parent. Attempting to control the child forces parent and child into oppositional roles, creating unmanageability in the home (Schaefer, 1982).

The alternative is to accept that no parent can completely protect his or her child all the time. As a parent you must accept that pain is not always a bad thing for your children to experience. Children will learn from pain. No amount of control will save your children from feeling some pain and hurt in their lives.

From this place of acceptance, you can share your love with your children and teach them to protect themselves. This will bring you closer to your children, helping to create harmony in your home. You can set the foundation for honest parenting by admitting that you are powerless over life and that trying manage your fear by controlling your child will not be successful.

STEP 2: *We came to believe that a power greater than ourselves could restore us to sanity.*

Find hope in the belief that recovery is possible through faith and a willingness to work on yourself.

An old adage says that a man can live three weeks without food and three days without water, but he cannot live three seconds without *hope*. The second step brings hope to the family affected by drug addiction. Drug-addicted families are filled with all kinds of learned insanity. The book *Twelve Steps and Twelve Traditions*, published by Alcoholics Anonymous (2004), defines sanity as soundness of mind. Whether you are a recovering drug addict, a spouse of a drug addict, or an adult child of a drug addict, who can honestly claim soundness of mind in the face of all the damage done by compulsive drinking, drugging, controlling, or eating? Any person from a dysfunctional family can identify behaviors that they call insane. These behaviors directly affect your parenting.

With the help of Step 2, you can develop the faith to leave these behaviors behind and create a new vision for yourself and your children. Faith is the beginning of hope. If you believe that a power greater than yourself can work in your life, then many miracles are possible.

STEP 3: *We made a decision to turn our will and our lives over to the care of God, as we understood God to be.*

Reach out for help and acknowledge that you are not alone.

In the third step, one learns to ask for help and let go of the need to have control over others. Asking for help is the lifeline for parents. Most people who come from drug-addicted homes don't know how to ask for help and are terrified to let go of their imagined control over their lives.

When you make a decision to turn your will and life over to the care of a Higher Power, you agree to do your share of the work but leave the worrying to someone else. All parents have moments in their lives when they think they are not going to make it through. For example, if your child were to run away, use drugs, become pregnant, or come down with a serious illness, you would need to draw on greater resources for strength. The third step makes these resources available to you for the big and little events in your life as a parent. Drawing on these resources and attempting to find *good orderly direction* (another name for a Higher Power) in your life will give you the sense of peace one needs to face the challenges of parenting. Allowing a concept of a Higher Power to lead you in your parenting will open up new avenues of inner knowledge that you didn't believe possible. When you turn your life over to a force greater than yourself, you also turn your children over. If you really let go of your need for control—if you step aside and let a force greater than yourself work in your life—you will find that your parenting becomes inspired.

STEP 4: *We made a searching and fearless moral inventory.*

Take stock of yourself as a parent.

The fourth step lets you own reality. It enables you to identify your strengths and weaknesses as a parent. While this may be an uncomfortable process at first, the rewards you will reap will make the effort more than worth the struggle. You need to examine where you do well and where you have problems parenting and why. This should be done without prejudgment. You are simply taking stock of your parenting warehouse and seeing what you have enough of and what you lack.

This will include a review of your personality traits and how they may affect your children. It is common for parents to project those aspects of themselves that they fear their children will act out, onto their children, thereby creating a self-fulfilling prophecy. This is often acted out by recovering drug-addicted parents who fear their children will do the things they did as children. Sometimes mothers who were promiscuous earlier in life will project sexual acting out on their daughters, when in fact their daughters are far less sexually active. The fourth step is a time to take responsibility for the things you don't like about yourself as opposed to projecting them onto your children.

Working through this step may also force you to face some upsetting facts about your parenting when you were actively drinking or using. It is important that you face the reality of your children's home life before you recovered so that you can avoid repeating past mistakes. This step is not intended to be a punishment; rather, its purpose is to give a clear picture of where you were, where you are now, and where you can go as an individual and as a parent. The Fourth Step is hard, but it opens the door to self-awareness and growth.

STEP 5: *We admitted to God, to ourselves, and to another human being the exact nature of our wrongs.*

Learn to share your parenting issues with others without self-recrimination.

Guilt is the great divider. It separates you from your loved ones. If you repress the baggage of the past, you are doomed to continue to carry it with you. Step 5 can liberate you as a parent. Once you have taken an inventory, you can see the exact patterns of behavior that get you into trouble with your spouse and children. Maybe it's perfectionism or fear of that sets you apart from your family. Whatever it is, until you admit to yourself, a Higher Power, and another human being, you will unwillingly carry the burden of unnecessary guilt with you.

This is also the sharing step, the time when you need to talk with your partner. Examine your parenting together. See what works for your family and what doesn't. By communicating, you can see what each of you can do to make your parenting more effective. With your spouse create a parenting team through an open and honest examination of your patterns of behavior as parents.

Step 5 allows you the opportunity to develop real honesty with other people. By sharing the things you see that you would like to change about your parenting with friends and members of your self-help group, you will find that you are not nearly as bad a parent as you thought you were and that you have all kinds of opportunities for support and guidance when you need them. This step allows you to drop the pretense of perfect parenting and allows you to join the rest of the world of imperfect people parenting imperfect people.

STEP 6: *We were entirely ready to have God remove all these defects of character.*

Become ready to change by giving up the demand to be perfect.

Be ready to *change*. Change is scary; it is not easy to become ready to change. Whatever patterns of behavior you have nurtured in the past, you nurtured for a reason. You may have done things in a particular way as a defense, to protect yourself or your self-esteem from being attacked or destroyed. Your defects are really the way the child in you protects itself from a hostile world. This is a poignant step. It asks you to parent the child within you in a new and different way. In order to become willing to change, you must face the child within and tell him or her that it is time to give up the old ways.

You will need to develop new ways to defend yourself when defense is necessary. You will need to find ways to protect your self-esteem that do not necessitate denying your feelings. Taking the sixth step means being ready to feel all your feelings as a parent and letting go of control as a way of defending yourself against feelings of vulnerability.

STEP 7: *We humbly asked God to remove our shortcomings.*

Make conscious changes in your parenting by identifying specific strategies for healthy parenting.

Becoming ready and humbly asking for your parenting shortcomings to be removed sets the stage for your *spiritual growth* as a parent. One of the chief problems that besets many drug addicts or people who grew up in drug-addicted families is self-righteousness. Step 7 is the great leveler.

In the seventh step you *ask* for help. This is not easy for people who have been affected by addiction. Generally speaking, one major symptom shared by compulsive people is an inability to ask for help. Asking for help with humility is even harder.

In this step you begin to make conscious changes of parenting techniques that are no longer effective. Your children will challenge these changes in you. You will need to let them know that you have discovered some ways to improve how you relate to one another and you are trying to apply them. Your children may even provoke you to get the old responses out of you. This is natural. You will need to set firm limits on their testing, but this is a period they will need to go through as you begin to remove the shortcomings in your parenting and as they adjust to your new style of parenting.

STEP 8: *We made a list of all persons we had harmed, and became willing to make amends to them all.*

Take responsibility for the effect your parenting has had on your children, and learn self-forgiveness.

This is a step in which you as a parent learn to forgive yourself. It will not be an easy matter. In Step 8 you will need to be very specific about the ways you harmed your children in the past and become willing to take responsibility for the past.

Accepting the past as a fact and *without guilt* is the way to do this step. This will be difficult. The natural reaction for parents looking back over a disturbing past history of parenting is either to judge themselves harshly or to minimize the effect they had on their children. We have seen parents who have said that their addictive or dependent behavior had no effect on their children. This is not true. By the same token, we have had parents come to see us who were sure they had done irreparable damage to their children. Fortunately, this is not true either.

Accepting responsibility is not the same as being guilty. If you are the adult child of a drug addict or alcoholic, it will be very easy for you to confuse guilt with responsibility. Taking responsibility for the past means that you accept the past for what it is. Commit to changing those behaviors that were harmful and follow through on your commitment. But taking responsibility means being ready to be very specific in admitting the truth about the past.

One way to simplify this step is to make a list of new parenting strategies you can implement. Making a list of the new strategies will give you a way out of guilt and a way into responsible action. Deciding how you will change as you face what it is you need to change and whom you need to change for, will release you from self-recrimination. Remember: no parent willfully hurts his child; most of what you do as a parent you learned from your parents, and no one is at fault. You need to recognize that you did the best you could at the time, and that now is the time to do better

Becoming a recovering parent is like becoming a recovering drug addict. Recovering drug addicts are not guilty or ashamed of their drug addiction because they are working on themselves to get healthier. You can let go of the shame and guilt associated with your past history as a parent by becoming a recovering parent who, like a recovering drug addict, accepts his problems and does something about them.

STEP 9: *We made direct amends to such people whenever possible, except when to do so would injure them or others.*

Make amends to your children through healthy parenting without overcompensating.

Making amends when the time is right will *support* your child in a special way. Many parents want to sit down and explain the past to their children as a way of making amends. This is not always advisable. In fact, any kind of open discussion of the past might best wait until your children are in their late teens or adults.

The best way to make amends to your children is by being a better parent. This is tricky for recovering drug addicts and ACoAs. The tendency for many who have had problems with parenting is to try to make up for lost time with their children. They attempt to become superparents to their kids as a means of assuaging their guilt about the past. This is not good for you or your children. Your children will sense the guilt behind your giving and they will not trust it. Or they may begin to manipulate you because of it, and then feel guilty for manipulating you. You do not have to be the best parent in town. You do need to commit yourself to being the best parent you can be. That is making amends.

Reading this book is making amends. It shows your *commitment* to learn more about helping your kids. Going to workshops or classes on parenting is making amends. Going to parent-teacher conferences is making amends. Being at the school play that your 6-year-old is in is making amends. Buying your child everything he or she asks for, or feeling like you must become a slave to your children's demands because you were a bad parent, is not making amends; that is doing penance.

Making amends as a parent should feel good to you. It means sharing your life and attention with your children. It means opening your family up to a healthy acceptance of each other's differences. It means giving permission for everyone to express feelings to one another. It means setting limits on your kids in a firm but loving manner. It means reaching inside yourself to heal the child in you who cries out for attention and love. It means becoming all that you were meant to be as a person and as a parent.

STEP 10: *We continued to take personal inventory and when we were wrong promptly admitted it.*

Model being honest with yourself and your children, and create acceptance of imperfection in your family.

This step is fundamental to becoming a healthy role model for your children. It is the step in which you as a parent give up your goal to be perfect and give your children permission to make mistakes. It is the self-honesty step. Here, you teach your children by your example that they can be imperfect and still be loved by you. That is an important lesson for children of addicts!

Children from drug-addicted homes often base their self-esteem on their performance. They learn from an early age not to make mistakes, and if they make mistakes, not to admit them. This is very damaging to the developing ego. Children learn by example. Most of what your children will take from you will come from them watching what you do, not following what you say. If you set healthy examples, your children will develop healthy ways of coping. Modeling daily self-honesty and self-acceptance will enable your children to learn to deal with life from a place in which their self-esteem is based, to paraphrase Dr. Martin Luther King, on the content of their character, not how close to perfect they can get.

STEP 11: *We sought, through prayer and meditation, to improve our conscious contact with God as we understood God to be, praying only for knowledge of God's will for us and the power to carry that out.*

Learn to accept your limits in life and find your true spiritual path while allowing your children theirs.

Spirituality is an important part of parenting. Children need an understanding of life based on spiritual principles, and they need values to live by. These values and principles should come from their parents. Develop a way of seeing life in a cosmic context so you can give your children a way to see the world. Families without clear spiritual values are often families that are drifting with no anchor. Spirituality means many different things to different people. There is no special direction you should take, but you need to find an expression of spiritual life for your family.

Step 11 is where you come to terms with the one essential painful truth about parenting: that in the end your children will be on their own, and that some *greater* plan exists for all of us. As Shakespeare said, we are all players in a grand play. Much of what happens around us we can't control. Letting go of what we can't control is the core of Step 11 as it relates to parenting.

There is a prayer around AA that goes like this: "God, thank you for all you have given me, for all you have taken away, and thank you for all you have left me." Many people who have grown up in homes where addiction is present have a hard time understanding that prayer. It is only after you have worked through the steps for a while that you will realize that your experiences as a child, even the very bad ones, have helped to make you who you are and that there is a lot of who you are that is good and positive and worth keeping. *Give thanks.*

By applying Step 11, you are able to draw on the guidance of your Higher Power on a daily basis. You allow yourself to be guided by a greater consciousness. This surrender to a power greater than yourself allows you to do your best as a parent and let go of the results. When you work through this step, you give your children up to a larger plan. You respect the fact that everyone must walk his or her own path and that you cannot control the choices your children will make in life.

You also open yourself up to recognizing your own path. At times, this may mean that your values clash with those around you. But in Step 11 we learn to trust the spiritual voice inside that dictates the choices we must make in order to live life with integrity. We learn true acceptance as a parent. You no longer try to control your children, but try instead to lead through guidance and example. Your children will no longer control you, because as you become more separate and self-validating, you will let go of the need for their approval. In this step, you learn to trust in a higher form of parenting that comes from understanding oneself in a spiritual context.

STEP 12: *Having had a spiritual awakening as the result of these steps, we tried to carry this message to drug addicts, and to practice these principles in all our affairs.*

Reach out to other parents in the spirit of giving and community.

There is another old saying in the 12-step programs: "You can't keep it unless you give it away." Sharing experience, strength, and hope is the cornerstone of these programs and the reasons why their members keep coming back. It is in helping others that one reaches the highest levels of recovery. For parents in recovery, this means reaching out to other parents in need and lending a hand.

This may mean sponsoring a parent in your self-help group, lending support and insight to others who are struggling in their recovery from drug addiction or learned helplessness to become better parents. It may mean establishing a parent support group in your community. Every parent needs support, not just those affected by addiction. Helping to organize a parent support group allows you to reach out to others who do not have the gift of the 12-step program.

For recovering parents, Step 12 certainly means getting involved in your children's schools. It may also mean getting involved with your community to establish or support recreation programs and substance abuse treatment and prevention programs. Carrying the message means that you become an example of concern and healthy parenting and that you learn to give of yourself freely when appropriate.

If you work through the 12-step programs to the best of your ability and face the challenges you encounter, you will become the parent you were meant to be—perhaps the parent you never had. You will learn how to give to the child within you all that he or she needs and lead your own children in a loving way. You can have it all, but the effort must be wholehearted and sincere. As the book *Alcoholics Anonymous* says, "rarely have we seen a person fail who has *thoroughly* followed our path."

Summary

Parenting is always a struggle between love and fear. Parents try to control their children in an attempt to protect them from any painful experiences. It is important to remember that the best you can do as a parent is be an example and encourage your children to their fullest by being all that you can be. As a recovering parent, you will need to take responsibility for learning about your children and developing new parenting strategies so that you may open new avenues of communication and self-respect in your families.

Finally, you need to follow the 12 Steps of Recovery, Revised for Parents:

Step 1: Admit powerlessness over your ability to protect your children from pain. Become willing to surrender to your love and not your control.

Step 2: Find hope in the belief that recovery is possible through faith and a willingness to work on yourself.

Step 3: Reach out for help and acknowledge that you are not alone.

Step 4: Take stock of yourself as a parent.

Step 5: Learn to share your parenting issues with others without self-recrimination.

Step 6: Become ready to change by giving up the demand to be perfect.

Step 7: Make conscious changes in your parenting by identifying specific strategies for healthy parenting.

Step 8: Take responsibility for the effect your parenting has had on your children and learn self-forgiveness.

Step 9: Make amends to your children through healthy parenting without over-compensating.

Step 10: Model being honest with yourself and your children, and create acceptance of imperfection in your family.

Step 11: Learn to accept your limits in life and find your true spiritual path while allowing your children theirs.

Step 12: Reach out to other parents in the spirit of giving and community.

CHAPTER 7

Parenting as a
Team/
Parenting
Alone

Parenting as a Team: Understanding Power Struggles

I used to wonder why we ever got married. We argued before we married, and argued even more after. When the kids came, our arguments turned into major campaigns against each other. We both felt trapped, especially me. How could I leave Sonia with an infant and a 2-year-old? I felt I should have left before we had kids. But here I was. I felt responsible for the lack of affection in my home. I withdrew from Sonia, just like Dad did from my mother. Sonia felt that we just couldn't make a go of it.

—Harry, 30, the adult child of a drug addict,
married to Sonia, 28, also an adult child of a
drug addict and a child incest survivor

Harry and Sonia are in a power struggle. Power struggles are part of many relationships. To have a power struggle does not always mean to be caught in one. Couples may go through periods of greater or lesser emphasis on power issues. How do you know you are in a power struggle? Power struggles occur when each person in a couple attempts to impose their personal view of the world on the other. If only one of you is right, or can be right, then you are in a power struggle.

The Impact of Addiction: How Power Struggles Develop

Family traditions provide a family with an identity. Special traditions can be anything: always naming the first baby girl after her mother, always eating pork on Christmas Eve, or even negative traditions such as the father coming home drunk on Friday night, or the mother and father fighting and waking up the family after using drugs. Wacky as they may seem, these traditions in a family system give the family's world predictability.

Power struggles in addicted families are almost certain. They develop from two major types of family traditions common in families where addiction is present: the tradition of having a closed family system that resists change and outside viewpoints, and the tradition of existing within a crisis-driven orientation.

The Closed Family System

Families affected by drug addiction tend to be closed families. In a closed family system, the family's unique set of rules functions as a protective shield from the rest of the world, and other points of view are stubbornly kept out. This means that little can change within the family. Change is frightening; it results in increased anxiety, and closed families, especially those where addiction is present, are already loaded with anxiety (Papp, 1983).

As children grow up, they learn how to function in their families, and they apply that knowledge to the rest of their experiences. In a closed family, children learn the "rules"—including how one should view the world and what constitutes love and intimacy—*only* as taught by their families. This is due, in part, to the isolation that the family lives in, isolation that effectively limits the exposure of the child to experiences outside the family (Wolin, Bennett, & Noonan, 1979).

Family members in a closed system develop and cling to highly personal ways of making sense of the world. This allows them to feel that there is cause and effect that they can influence, and that is predictable, even if it is painful. Predictable pain is often easier to bear than unpredictable change. To maintain this illusion of control, family members rely increasingly on their family's way of doing and perceiving things. Unconsciously, they begin to derive much of their personal identity from their family's approach to the world. The more they cling to how their family has consciously and unconsciously taught them to see the world and to interpret the actions of others, the more dependent they learn to be. Unless they are exposed to other experiences, this personalized worldview will become fixed and limiting; the rigidity and resistance to change may itself become a family rule. As they begin to form close relationships outside of the family, they maintain their particular view of the world and their place within it, and will fight anyone who attempts to counter it.

Part of recovery is change. Change is difficult for everyone, and therefore people tend to resist it. If only one member of the couple is recovering, change can be particularly onerous. Many people in recovery from addiction, or from the effects of living with an addict, become caught in power struggles with a loved one as they change the rules of the relationship. In time, however, some couples in recovery begin to have enough distance from the dynamics of their relationship to allow them to see their relationship more clearly, less emotionally, and to realize that they have been involved in power struggles all along (Steinglass et al, 1993).

Crisis Orientation

Families affected by drug addiction rock along from crisis to crisis. These crises are often triggered by power struggles within the family—that is, one family member wanting another to behave in a certain way and not accepting an alternative behavior or viewpoint—which are usually a product of a closed family system.

When a crisis occurs in a family where addiction is a factor, each person's role is clearly defined, and everyone can predict how the others in the family will act, for each part has been rehearsed many times before. It is almost as if a fire alarm has sounded, and each person dutifully reports to his or her battle station. This type of crisis-driven behavior can lend order to a chaotic family. Indeed, in such families, members often communicate better and more thoroughly when they are in crisis than when they are not. Contact and emotional closeness, even in a negative context, are emotional gains that keep the family generating crises so that they will communicate with one another and have some predictability in their lives.

By contrast, in noncrisis times, family members may be distant, isolated, and even alienated from each another. Family members may have no understanding of their roles in times of calm, and so the family drifts with no way of creating intimacy until the next crisis. Therefore, family members affected by drug addiction often sustain a series of traumas as a way to maintain intimacy. The family often organizes around these crises, and behaving in a predictable, almost prescribed—but painful—manner (Bowen, 1974). Harry provides an example:

> I remember my first intellectual battle with my father. He was drunk and asked me what I was studying. I told him mammals. He then quizzed me on what makes an animal a mammal, and he was wrong. I even showed him in my textbook, but he said that they were wrong, and I was stupid for believing them. So we battled over whether the textbook and my teacher were correct. He just couldn't accept any other point of view but his own. Looking back on it, these battles were the only times my Dad and I would speak.

Power Struggles, Addiction, and Parenting

Power struggles often emerge when relationships are formed between two individuals from closed family systems, as two personal worldviews clash, and as each tries to defend against the anxiety represented by allowing in the other's viewpoint

(Campbell, 1984). Seeing the world from only one perspective would work fine if you lived alone on a desert Island. But it doesn't work in a relationship, and it doesn't work for parenting. It is important to remember that operating in crisis is a comfortable and familiar way for addicts to behave. If you and your spouse recognize this pattern in your behavior, you need to learn new ways of handling problems and creating intimacy.

Children also complicate and intensify existing power struggles. Parents will watch to see whose view their children will adopt, their mother's or father's. In adopting one parent's view, the children also validate it, something one parent may use against the other parent to the detriment of the children.

The Triple Bind

Many of those affected by addiction become engaged in power struggled by becoming trapped in a classic "triple bind." These tangled webs of attitudes about power were often unconsciously developed as a response to dealing with the crisis-orientation found in addicted families.

- *Those affected by addiction can become fixed in the past.* They fear the past will repeat itself. Often, they inadvertently help recreate their past in the present, and in this way they create the illusion of control. Again, predictable pain is more bearable than unpredictable change

- Sometimes, in an effort to learn how well they can cope, *they create their own worst nightmares as a means of proving to themselves—and to others— that they can survive under any circumstances.* Some have such high anxiety concerning what *could* happen that they try to control their fate by making it happen instead of letting it happen. This can be anything from an argument to a divorce.

- *They may have ungrounded fears of failure.* They may fear that the future will not hold success for them, that they will not grow personally, or that their children will not progress. They may feel cursed, that nothing will ever work out for them. They can become trapped in obsessing about all the terrible things that can happen, and planning how they will deal with them.

- *They may fear success.* Many children from addicted homes unconsciously fear that if they are successful, they will lose their family's love. They are terrified of being different, and therefore being rejected by their families. This is often disguised as a fear of failure. Failure is often more acceptable within the family system than success. The hidden clue that this is occurring is that the individual creates elaborate precautions to actually avoid, or even sabotage, their own success. If, despite all their efforts and precautions, the person still manages to be successful, he or she will minimize it, invalidate it, or otherwise not enjoy it, because they will think of it as is fleeting.

When two people who have different and fixed worldviews form a relationship, these personalized worldviews create conflicts. This is because each person acts and interprets the other's actions from the confines of their own rigid perspective. This results in couples who do not, for example, ask what is bothering the other, but who assume that they not only know what their partner is feeling, but why, and whose fault it is. This clash of worldviews means that neither partner feels loved, and in fact, both people may doubt that they know *how* to love their spouse, or even their children. Since there is little communication in the presence of power struggles, there is much misinterpretation, and few, if any, opportunities for new input that would challenge these views.

Negotiating the Power Struggle
From Win/Lose Thinking to Both/And Thinking

The type of reasoning that lies behind a power struggle is called "win/lose" thinking, because either you or your spouse must be 100% right, and one must be completely wrong. Both of you cannot be validated. Responsibility in a win/lose situation is not shared, just as in a family where there is active drug addiction. In fact, no one wants to assume responsibility, and so it is thrown about like a hot potato. Each party fights to exempt themselves from being wrong, and so must make the other wrong. Harry explains:,

> When I could discuss anything with Sonia, it was obvious that only one of us could be right. Having kids made this crystal clear. Women in her family were always right concerning the children. Men in my family were always wrong, and knew nothing about childrearing. We were a perfect dysfunctional fit. When I decided that I didn't like this and needed to do something, I rebelled just like I did as a kid. I began to push for things that weren't even that important to me just because I didn't want to lose another round to her and be a wimp like my father, the passive drug addict.

One way to resolve a power struggle is to move from "win/lose" thinking to "both/and" thinking. Including both points of view and taking the best from each is a way of stepping around a power struggle and redefining the struggle from "win/lose" to "win/win" (Campbell, 1984). Harry elaborates:

> It was not so easy to do, but possible. Things were really getting out of hand with the kids; we had to do something. How did I do it? Really, we did it.

The authors have found that couples usually manage to negotiate their power struggles in the following manner:

Accept Your Spouse

Acceptance, the essence of the first step of all 12-step recovery programs, is crucial to redefining a power struggle. Accept your spouse. You have made a commitment to him or her, and have gone through many rough times already. These difficult times have forged and strengthened your relationship, so if you can, let go and accept. Harry illustrates this:

> I began to see Sonia's need to define my role as distinct from childrearing as her way of remaining close to her family traditions that said "don't trust men around children." This made sense when I remembered that she was an incest survivor. And she needed to see herself as a good mother and not be like her own mother, ineffective in protecting her children. Instead of always being angry with her, I began to see her great love of our children, and to deeply appreciate her need to protect them. In accepting her, I realized that I did love her, something that in my righteous anger I had lost sight of. In my family, love was always replaced by anger. It occurred to me that I had been carrying on that tradition.

Change Your Interpretations of Your Spouse's Actions

You can only change yourself. Begin by owning your personal view of the world. Understand how you want to be seen and be willing to entertain how your spouse wants to be seen. This small step will produce a marked change in your relationship. Harry says,

> I realized that I couldn't change Sonia, and maybe I didn't have to, if I could see what was really motivating her, instead of judging her from my point of view. First I changed how I interpreted her actions. These same actions under a different heading seemed fine. A bit quirky, but that's Sonia.
>
> Next I accepted her and released her from my constant criticism. Interestingly, as I backed off, Sonia become more verbal about her worries about the children and acted them out less. I became less of the enemy, which meant, of course, that I had to be willing to give up this role, and risk getting closer to Sonia. To give up my role, I first had to realize I had the power to change myself.

Change Your Own Actions

After you have realized the legitimacy of your spouse's view, you can decide what you want to do, knowing that you have the power to change yourself. This means taking responsibility for you and you alone. Not an easy task, as Harry observes:

How to change me? It was easier to do after I stopped putting all my energy into changing her. I began with how I reacted around the kids. I accepted Sonia's need to protect them. But I also stopped acting so inadequate around them, like my father had. This meant that I stopped sending Sonia the message that I couldn't handle them, and that they needed to be protected from my bumbling. My changing my actions, and accepting hers, resulted in a big change. We stopped battling so much. We moved from "either/or" thinking to "both/and" thinking. It is great to be in a relationship where you both emerge as winners.

Some Guidelines for Moving Beyond the Power Struggle

Once you have negotiated the power struggle, you need to recommit to each other. Commitment can be a challenge, because it involves learning some new behaviors. But this can be seen as the next necessary step in the lifelong process of recovery. Harry began to close the gap between how he wanted to be seen and how Sonia was seeing him.

Develop Active Listening Skills

- Train yourself to actively listen to your partner's feelings before you respond. If anything is unclear, ask.

- Actively learn more about your partner—her fears, hopes, and insights regarding your children, your marriage, yourself.

Plan Time Together

- Plan times to be together away from the children. Even an hour here or there can work wonders.

- Pick a weekly time to review issues that concern your children. Let at least part of this time be away from the children.

Negotiate Differences

- Respect the different values of your spouse. After all, if you agreed on everything, you would be the same person.

- If a decision is not as important to you as it is to your spouse, let it pass. Let him have it his way. And don't go back and say, "I told you so" if there are problems.

- Learn to defer judgment on a problem if either of you is too tired to process it.

Develop Clear Expectations Together

For your children, regarding:

- appropriate behavior;

- expected behavior, i.e., chores;

- consequences for inappropriate behavior; and

- rewards and other ways to motivate your children.

For yourselves as parents, regarding:

- What role each of you is willing to play with the children.

Yourselves as a couple, paying close attention to:

- What translates into love for each of you; and

- How to show your partner, in a way that he or she understands, that he or she is loved.

Negotiating power issues is not a one-time event, and it is never easy. You will need to pay constant attention to this area of your development. Remember that growth is not linear. You will go back and forth, and have spurts and setbacks. Even trees do not grow even bands each year. So be gentle with each other as you grow and love together.

Parenting Alone

Sometimes recovery can involve stays in drug rehabilitation facilities, which may not be close to home. At other times, whether from the effects of the disease alone, or due to other factors, a partnership may end in separation, divorce, or even death. Whatever the circumstances, this means learning to parent alone.

Losing a husband or wife, even temporarily, deprives you of the opportunity of working through problems with your partner. Parenting alone is hard in the best of circumstances; it's even harder for a family affected by drug abuse.

Parenting alone presents the same issues as parenting with a spouse. Certainly the child's developmental issues are the same. The child needs the same amount of structure, support, and consistency. The difference is that you are now only one, as opposed to two, trying to provide for your children.

You need support, support, and more support. Not only do you need it, but you deserve it as well. Support can come from many sources. They range, depending on your needs, from week- or day-long family programs at the drug-addiction treatment facility, to professional help, to your 12-step program (where the topic of parenting alone would spark a lively discussion), to other self-help organizations, such as Parents Without Partners.

Remember that living with drug addiction and other addictions teaches one to live alone. You need to break free of this and reach out to others. Don't isolate yourself or your children.

Blended Families

Where children are involved, divorce is marriage in another form, for now a lifelong relationship exists with the ex-spouse through the children. Remarriages and live-in arrangements, where children are present, are called *blended families*, because each adult represents a parental figure. This need not mean that the child calls both women "Mother," or both men "Father." A child will often resist that, with good cause. It does mean, however, that the child now has more adults to love and to please in his or her life.

In the best of circumstances, blended families can become strong sources of support for the children as well as the adults. But loyalties may become divided and painful for the child, particularly when biological parents are involved in power struggles. It is important to remember that even when parents are not outwardly struggling, a child feels torn. At some level he wants Mommy and Daddy to be back together. This is a normal, largely unconscious, and—at least from the parents' point of view—irrational desire by the child, which the adults in his or her life will need to accept.

Parenting under these circumstances is difficult, but not because the child wants it to be. It is unavoidable, not least because there are just that many more people involved in the child's life, and that many more people involved in yours.

Everything that has been said about the power struggles occurring within a marriage goes double for a blended family. Eliminating these power struggles and working to develop communication are crucial if harmony within the family and within the marriage is to be established.

Some special issues within the blended family need to be addressed. These again are issues of power struggles compounded by guilt. The authors have found these issues can be addressed successfully, once they are understood.

Double Standards

There should not be two sets of standards, one for those children who reside with you, and one for those children who spend weekends and/or summers. This is difficult to accomplish, but necessary. There must be rules for all the children to follow, and rewards and consequences. It is recommended that the rules govern expectations that occur only during the times the child is with you. The issue here is that the behavior and its accompanying reward and consequences must be able to be accomplished over the weekend or summer.

For example, taking away bike riding for a month for a child who only spends every other weekend with you is not a good idea. When the child returns in two weeks, having ridden his bike at the other parent's home in between, your grounding him will seem more mean, than meaningful, as too much time will have elapsed.

In cases of serious behavioral problems, where there is a good relationship between the separated parents, exceptions can be made, and punishment can be coordinated between the two sets of parents. But you and the child must be very clear as to what this exception is and why it is happening.

Who Is In Charge?

Another complication that arises when a child has double parents, and parents have double sets of children, is the question of who makes the rules for which children. Who is in charge? In some families, power can be shared, even with the children. Here the parenting as a team approach can and does work well. In other families, guilt, or apathy on the part of the nonbirthparent, frequently interferes, and only the birthparent makes the rules or enforces them.

To determine which style will work for you, you need to have some serious conversations with your partner. It is recommended that you try to clarify who has what role with which children. This will not only help you, but it makes that child's life easier and more secure as well. For children, security comes from predictability.

Summary

Learning to be a good parent can be part of the recovery process. Parenting as a team means working through power struggles found within the marriage, and then getting down to the business of negotiating how to be the parent that your children need, and that you would like to be. Partners who are separated—whether it be permanent or temporary—and blended families only compounds power struggles. Accepting your spouse and yourself provides the important first steps in renegotiating power issues.

CHAPTER 8

Preparing for
Birth and Parenting
the Infant

Today I brought my son Eshawn to the babysitter. He was crying. He started his day so upset. I vowed that if I ever became a parent that I would never do to my child what my parents did to me. Why? Why am I doing just what I was afraid I would do?

—Aretha, 32, an adult child of a drug addict and
an active drug addict; married to Gary, son of a drug addict
who was also a compulsive gambler

Preparing for Birth

Just making the decision to have a child raises anxiety in those who have been affected by drug addiction and other addictions. Being pregnant raises yet additional concerns. How to prepare for a coming child? It is important to remember this: "Virtually everything you consume or inhale while pregnant will be passed through to the fetus. This process begins as soon as you conceive. In fact, the embryo is most vulnerable during the first two months, when the major body parts are just starting to form" (Shelov, 1998, p. 4).

You can increase the likelihood of having a healthy baby by:

- following a healthy, balanced diet, with no bingeing or purging,

- not drinking alcohol or caffeine,

- not using illegal drugs or nicotine,

- not misusing any prescription or over-the-counter drugs, and

- following a healthy exercise program.

No single action will ensure the health of your baby, but if you eat healthy foods in a responsible manner and cease to use alcohol, drugs, caffeine, and/or nicotine, you will know that you are doing everything possible to help your baby. Remember, no one can guarantee the health of your baby. Genetics and age of the parents are also important variables in determining the health of your child. All we are speaking about here is controlling what is in your power to control—not an insignificant task for recovering people.

Aside from proper diet and exercise, reading and speaking to other parents will help prepare you for what might occur. In preparing for birth you need to have faith in yourself, your partner, and your support programs. Learn to relax and enjoy the process, and after the child is born, follow the simple rules outlined in this chapter.

Parenting Infants and Addiction

Taking care of an infant can feel like an overwhelming task for someone who has been affected by drug addiction. Infants are so fragile and require so much attention that the very purity of their vulnerability can elicit fear, resentment, and feelings of inadequacy in a mother or father who did not receive adequate care themselves. Aretha illustrates:

> I feel sometimes that I have been cursed by my family. When I had my first child and asked my mother for help, she said, "You'll learn." But she never told me how to care for my baby. Didn't she realize that I had no experience to draw upon? I had to do this all alone, just like I grew up—all alone. I resented it and, God forgives me, I also resented my child. If Eshawn didn't get my wrath, Gary, my husband, would.

The Young Infant: Under 6 Months

RULE: *Parents need to provide their infant with a calm, predictable, consistent, and loving environment.*

Studies have shown that children in the early stages of life need to feel special, loved, and valued. They need to feel safe and confident about what to expect from their environment. They need guidance and a balanced experience of freedom and limits. And they need to be exposed to a diverse environment filled with language play, exploration, books, music, and appropriate toys (Shelov, 1998). This may seem like a tall order, maybe even an impossible one. But it is manageable if you approach each task one at a time, one day at a time!

Guidelines

- *Predictability is not rigidity.* Predictability for infants means learning that when they cry, they will be comforted. This does not mean that comfort must come immediately or even every time. There are valid philosophies of child rearing, for example, that state that it may be appropriate for infants of a certain age to cry themselves to sleep after they have been fed and changed. Predictability only means that the child can look forward to being comforted and develop an expectation that it will occur.

- *Consistency is also not rigidity.* It does not mean that every time an infant is comforted, it must be done the same way. Consistency means that there are limits that the nurturing falls within, and that it always falls within these limits.

- *Calm is not the absence of stimulation.* Calm is stimulation that the child can absorb, stimulation that does not overpower the child and frighten him or her. Children are very adaptable. They can get used to different levels of stimulation. How much stimulation a child needs depends in part on the personality present at birth. It also depends on the normal activity level of their family. To have a totally calm environment is impossible. Doors will slam; voices may occasionally be raised. This is normal. It is nonetheless important to strive to have a calm environment. Remember, however, that too much stimulation will scare a child, and one of your main tasks as a parent is to help the child feel safe and special.

- *It is very difficult not to love an infant.* It is, however, possible to have difficulty in showing your love. Part of this difficulty may come from feelings of competition with one's child. Gary admits:

  > I used to feel that this kid had a lot more than I did. It would make me feel sad—sad for me. I began to wish that I had me for a father. I began to resent that Eshawn had it so good. This really got in the way of how I cared for Eshawn until I realized what was going on.

It is important to remember that love can be shown in many ways that we sometimes do not think of as loving. Smiles, a laugh, a bottle full of warm milk, a toy, a touch—all are ways we show our love. However we express them, our feelings are not lost on infants. Infants process the world through their feelings. They can sense yours. Conscious and cognitive thoughts, as we shall see, come later.

Given this world of love, relative calm, predictability, and consistency, the infant sets about to accomplish his development. One of the first tasks that the infant learns is how to alleviate the pain of hunger. Instinctively, infants vocalize and move about. Eventually they learn that they can produce an end to their hunger pains by these actions. This is a crucial point. The infant is learning that she can reduce her pain and influence her world. This is the beginning of the child's developing a sense of mastery over herself and her environment.

By nurturing the child, the mother and father bond to the child, and the infant in turn bonds with its parents. Bonding is important for both parents and the child. Bonding allows the child to feel secure. Security for the infant is experienced as a sense of order and predictability. Bonding allows the parents to begin to feel that they know what they are doing, to develop a sense of mastery that will be the cornerstone of their later parenting. Bonding with a child also allows a parent to feel that the commitment they have made to the child is worthwhile. After all, parenting is hard work. If you don't feel close to your child, it's much more difficult.

The Impact of Addiction

Love, consistency, and predictability are the important parenting tasks. The very nature of drug addiction makes following this rule difficult. Drug addiction causes personality changes that result in parents being unpredictable (Wallace, 1985). Emotional blowups are more common with people raised in alcoholic homes. Anger within the family can shatter the calm that all parents would like to be able to give their child.

What drug addiction does not affect, however, is the love the parent has for their child. It only affects how this love is demonstrated. The devastating part of drug addiction is that it robs both parent and child. Addicted parents are robbed of feelings of mastery and competence. They are also denied an outlet for their love.

Children are affected by drug addiction on many levels. Infants from homes where addiction is present often have difficulty being calm and anticipating that their needs will be met—that is, learning to trust. Just because a child comes from a home with drug addiction does not mean that he or she is scarred for life. It just means that certain tasks will be more difficult. For example, learning how to trust.

As noted in the previous chapter, children do learn to trust. To be untrusting and to be an infant means to die. We saw this in studies of English children separated from their parents for months during World War II. Here large numbers of otherwise healthy infants died, for they had no hope. They received virtually no individual love, no touching, and no cuddling, predictable or not. They gave up and died (Spitz & Wolf, 1946). This is the extreme. No one reading this book fell into this category or you would not be here today.

Infants are resilient. They fight to live, to grow, to master, even when the odds are against them. Despite intermittent caring or the ravages of wars, famine, or natural disasters, children can and do survive and thrive. Trust is not an all-or-nothing phenomenon. Likewise, children who grow up in homes where addiction is present— a situation that bears certain parallels with the desperate scenarios above—do learn to trust. But they learn a different type of trust, one in which the verdict is out longer as to whether trust has been earned. The child consequently takes longer to grant trust. Some children may learn to trust only themselves, excluding others as untrustworthy. This may lead to later antisocial behavior (Mussen, Conger, & Kagan, 1969).

For children of drug addicts, difficulty in trusting and in the relative lack of calm has ramifications for later life. As Aretha tells us:

> I felt so inadequate in trying to give my children something I had not experienced. Somehow I felt like a fake. I acted calm, but inside I was terrified. I prayed that it wouldn't show. One thing I am proud of is that somehow I did manage to be predictable, at least when Eshawn was an infant.

Remember, both parents do not have to be available at the same time for the child to grow. Even if your spouse cannot be a more predictable, consistent, calm, or outwardly loving parent, you should not give up. Do the best you can to achieve these goals. Children are adaptable. All a child minimally requires is one caretaker at a time. This does put an added stress on the more consistent caretaker, but you can manage this stress with support from 12-step programs, friends, and family.

RULE: *Parenting is trial and error.*

There is no easy way to learn to be a parent. This is hard for perfectionists to accept. For someone who has been affected by addiction, not knowing usually increases anxiety. You need to accept that you will not have all the answers ahead of time. No parent does.

The Importance of Information

Several tried-and-true methods have been developed over generations to reduce the natural anxiety of parenting. Information gathering is one way. By obtaining information from your doctor, friends, or other authorities, you can test your reactions to some classic situations such as preparing for childbirth. Reading about parenting will provide you with some of the basics. Experience also helps. Even if you grew up in a drug-addicted home, your previous experience with young children can quell some of your anxiety. Finding a support network is another important means of gathering information, as well as finding support and assistance. This is why, in many cultures, a married woman lives close to her mother. Her mother and other female family members are there with the knowledge and support she needs to help rear her children. There's a rule to be learned here: do not isolate yourself. But when you have learned to live with drug addiction, this is easier said than done. It may require you to break the family tradition of isolation to reach out to other mothers and fathers and develop friendships. Make the effort.

Learning from Your Baby

Most of what you will learn about yourself as a parent and about your child will come from actual experience and from your ability to learn from your experiences. Being spontaneous and not taking yourself too seriously are important lessons. Once you begin to become freer with your experiences and less judgmental, you will be able to interact more with your infant and enjoy him or her more. Learning more about your baby and yourself also promotes parent-child bonding.

It is common to overreact to your infant in the beginning, when you are tired or under stress. It is also common to underreact, only to find out later that your baby has kicked off all the covers and is cold and crying. Your reactions to your infant will never be perfect, so there is no reason to feel guilty when you discover a missing cover, or a cut or a bruise. What is important is how you handle the situation, not how you were inadvertently responsible for it. Many new parents are tempted to feel eternal guilt. Watch this pattern of guilt as it is probably more reflective of your overall personality style than it is an appropriate response to the situation. You may also want to try to check this reaction early so that you do not sow the seeds for taking on too much responsibility onto yourself. Learning from your children means learning to forgive yourself. As you get closer to your child and understand your manner of responding and fulfilling his or her needs, you will begin to develop more self-confidence.

Mothers who begin to know their children can often predict and interpret their early nonverbal behavior. Often, mothers and fathers who are primary caretakers will begin to tell that their baby is hungry or needs to be changed just by a change of tone in a cry, or a subtle action on their baby's part. Food preferences are another area of potential anxiety, especially as you begin to introduce solid food to your baby's diet (McCall, 1979). Anxiety over food can be subtly transmitted. Try to avoid perceiving the rejection of food as the rejection of the food provider; just because your son is rejecting strained peaches does not mean he is rejecting you. Gradually, by trial and error, you will learn your child's needs and preferences (hopefully before they change them on you again). This knowledge is based on trial and error, spending time with the child, and frequently misinterpreting their infant's communications until a pattern is discerned.

Unfortunately, drug addiction interferes with this natural trial-and-error learning process. As previously mentioned, many addicts are themselves the adult children of addicts—or had chaotic childhoods for other reasons—so they often have very little experience to draw on in terms of learning a positive parenting style. In addition, the person who is under the influence does not usually learn from any experiences he or she has while intoxicated (Wallace, 1985). Consequently, the mastery of parenting tasks is delayed. For example, learning to predict why the baby is crying will take longer. This results in increased stress for the child and parent and an increase in the length of time it will take the child to bond with the parent who is the primary caregiver (McCall, 1979).

Learning is also hampered for the spouse of a drug addict because the addict's neediness often conflicts with the needs of their children. If this happens, the children's needs will be met less consistently.

The adult child of a drug addict presents a different dilemma. These parents may tend to doubt their own instincts. They tend to be overanxious parents who are afraid that they will miss something with their child. They often become hyperattentive (Black, 1981; Gravitz & Bowden, 1985). In fact, these parents can become so attentive that they miss quite a bit by creating such an air of anxiety that the child senses this and responds to the anxiety instead of the parent.

Martin, 24, has been married for two years and has a 2-month-old girl. Martin is the adult child of a drug addict and suffers from being a compulsive overeater. Many of the arguments he has with Terri, his wife, have to do with his anxiety concerning Crystal, their daughter. The fact that she is thriving and growing on breast milk is not enough for Marty. He goes with Terri to doctor's appointments so that he can personally ask the questions that keep him awake and eating until all hours of the night. Gradually, Marty is learning what is normal for Crystal. Terri is also beginning to learn that Marty's questioning of her stems from his anxiety, and is not a comment on her mothering. She is learning not to personalize all of Marty's anxieties.

Drug addiction and related problems have a tendency to make parents feel that they must be perfect to ensure that their children will not become addicts. As Aretha said, "I feared that if I didn't do everything just right, Eshawn would grow up to be a mess."

Be reassured that no parent is—or can be—perfect. Better to put your energies into enjoying your baby and delighting in her accomplishments and your own, rather than directing all your energies into mulling over the way you were raised.

The Older Infant: 6 to 8 Months

As a child grows, he begins to assert what he wants. Not only do children have dis-
tinct preferences at this age, but also they begin to change physically and to look
distinctive. Parents begin to realize that they are dealing with another person, which
may cause them to feel as though they are losing control. As Aretha relates:

> *Changes were gradual with Eshawn. Then one day, I realized that he wasn't just a doll for
> me to feed and put to bed. He was beginning to talk. He recognized me, was afraid of
> strangers, and wouldn't smile on command. I got scared all over again. I felt again that I
> didn't have as much control as I needed.*

RULE: *Parents need to accept that children of both sexes
will probably have an initial strong bond with their mothers.*

The reason for this strong maternal-child bond is that the mother tends to be
the primary caretaker, especially for newborns. The mother is often the first person the child can depend upon and communicate with to have his or her basic
needs met. Since most of the comforting and nurturing has been provided by the
mother, when the child is upset, he will seek out the parent he knows will understand and take care of him. This will change as the child gets older and has more
experiences with the father and other adult caretakers, but it is important to remember that this early attachment is natural and normal, not a statement concerning who is the better or favored parent. It is only a statement on who is more familiar to the child and with whom the child can communicate with more readily
(Schaeffer, 1971).

The Impact of Addiction

Aretha, the adult child of drug addict parents, helps us see that this mother-child
bond can be double-edged:

> *I felt so actively ambivalent with Eshawn's strong ties to me. Part of me felt great: I was so
> important to him. That meant I was important, period. But since I had crossed Gary out
> of Eshawn's life because I was "the one," I also felt overwhelmed and unsupported.*

A child's strong ties with his mother can set up dynamics with far-reaching ripples
within the addicted family. Fathers often have a difficult time with young children.
Part of the reason is the trouble some men have in delighting in a preverbal, dependent being. Gary explains:

> *There just wasn't enough of a person there for me to interact with and feel satisfied. I also
> was so frightened that I would hurt him. But that was just part of the reason I had a*

difficult time with Eshawn. I also felt rejected because Aretha and Eshawn seemed to have their thing going, and I was excluded. For a long time whenever Eshawn cried, only Aretha could comfort him. I felt useless and left out, just like when I was a kid. When Aretha began to drink more heavily, I didn't know what to do, since I wasn't part of their world anyway, so I withdrew.

This normal process of a close bonding between mother and child also results at times in the inability of fathers to show as much initiative in caring for children. While some women have little difficulty with this in the beginning, after the child is older and the father is still not actively involved, resentments emerge in relation to the mother's feelings that she has to "do it all."

The parent with one or more active addictions also has difficulty with this phase of parenting. An addicted father may see child's natural initial preference for mother as a rejection of him, and not as a natural phase of development. He may later feel guilty in recovery that somehow he caused this natural event to occur. His partner may feel the same resentments and fears expressed by Aretha—power, but with too much responsibility. An addicted mother may experience her child's dependence on her as excessive. This dependence may heighten her sense of inadequacy, in that she has to pretend to know what to do. Her fear is that if she somehow falters, the world will cave in. This fear may even lead her to increased alcohol use to deaden her fears, as it did with Aretha.

The mother/child bonding may contribute to adult children of addicts feeling that they have to do everything and do it alone. Aretha says:

Somehow being a mother made me again feel if I didn't do it, it wouldn't get done. Suddenly I had to control everything all over again. Gary just wasn't there. And I blamed him for leaving me hanging. What I wasn't aware of was that I had pushed Gary away. I hadn't helped him create a role with Eshawn, particularly when Eshawn would only be comforted by me. I see now that I should have at least asked Gary to comfort me. I loved being so powerful with Eshawn, yet I resented both Eshawn and Gary for the enormity of the responsibility I felt.

Enjoying Your Baby

Having a baby is a mutual responsibility. How you choose to divide child care will depend on your other priorities. The important issue is to decide who is going to do what with your baby. The following are some guidelines to assist you:

- Decide together who has certain child care tasks.

- Try to take turns doing some aspects of child care.

- Share your experiences and those of your infant with one another.

- If you have older children, let their care be as important as your infant's. If they are old enough, determine whether they can safely participate in some aspect of infant care.

- Remember, you will learn as you go if you get the support that you need.

- If you develop resentment toward your child—e.g., you begin believe your infant will have a better life than you because they have you as a parent—do some parenting for yourself. Be good to yourself, and you will have fewer instances of resenting your baby. If resentments persist, you may want to speak to a professional.

- Love your baby as much as you can. There is no limit to the amount of love that a baby can absorb.

Summary

Parenting is a learned skill. No one was born knowing how to be a parent; rather, skillful parenting develops from trial and error. This means you will make mistakes, and you will need to learn to forgive yourself. Remember that you cannot do it all at once. Familial drug addiction may have influenced the development of your parenting skills, but it does not have to affect your ability to learn or to love. As you try some new techniques, don't try to be perfect. That's both impossible and a waste of time. Better to put your energy into enjoying and loving your baby and appreciating his or her accomplishments: learning to walk, to speak, and to be like Mommy and Daddy. Enjoy your ability to give to your child, and celebrate your mastery over what you have overcome to get here.

CHAPTER 9

Parenting the
Toddler and Preschool
Child

Monique is so ambivalent. One minute she wants me, and then she'll push me away and have a temper tantrum when I go near her. I feel like such a failure.

—Holly, age 23, an ACoA, and an alcoholic

Parenting the Toddler: 18 Months to 3 Years

Toddlers are in the process of emerging as autonomous people. Not only are they now learning to move on their own, but toddlers are also learning to express themselves verbally, beginning to deal with their need for independence, and learning to control their bodily functions. Gone is the very special mother-child relationship in which only the mother knew that the child wanted or needed and where only the mother could comfort the child. The child may now go to either parent for comforting, although a preference for the mother may still exist. The toddler makes his or her desires known, at times more than the parents wish, hence the description of toddlerhood as "the terrible twos." Wolin and Wolin (1992) call this the age of *optimistic exploring* because the child feels capable of moving into life. The child expresses this by having firm opinions, as they tend to state frequently in form of the word "NO!," a favorite of 2-year-olds. This is a time when children discover the concept of selfhood, or "I," and use this to gain power and influence over their parents and their environment.

RULE: *Parents need to foster their child's need for independence.*

According to Shelov (1998), children at this age alternate between emphatically stating their independence to the point that many parents feel caught in a battle wills, to clinging to their parents and being afraid of strangers. For the toddler, there is a push/pull quality to feelings of independence. Sometimes it is okay to be independent, and sometimes it is not. The toddler dramatically exhibits this by running over to his mother to be comforted, and when she responds, pushing her away. The toddler both wants and doesn't want to be independent. He is experimenting with how different responses feel and how successful one response is over another in meeting his needs.

Fostering Independence and Avoiding Learned Helplessness

Again, consistency on the part of the parents is important, particularly when the child is inconsistent. The child needs to know that he will not be punished for wanting to do things on his own. If parents are inconsistent during this period, the child may well become excessively dependent on his parents. Probably the easiest way to ensure the development of excessive dependence in a child is to reward an activity one time and punish it the next. This can teach the child not to trust his own impulses.

For example, a child may be punished for sucking her thumb by a parent under the influence. The other parent may encourage the child to suck her thumb when the addicted parent is intoxicated as a way of letting the child reduce her stress. The same activity when the addicted parent is not intoxicated may go unnoticed by both parents.

This, in the authors' experience, is the reason why adult children of alcoholics who feel so frightened by independence often develop compulsively dependent relationships. Adult children of addicts may unconsciously reason that if they are dependent on someone else, then they do not need to risk being vulnerable and potentially punished for their own decisions. If you never make decisions for yourself but only make decisions for others, then you can be safe.

Encouraging independence is difficult for the addicted parent, because this taps into the addict's own ambivalence over his lack of independence from the source of his addiction (Wallace, 1985). Active drug addicts have not yet decided that they want independence.

> *When I think of Sun Hei moving toward self-sufficiency, I'm really amazed. I feel I haven't yet completed this process, and I know Mee Na hasn't.*
>
> —Jeon Wok, an adult child of an addict; married to Mee Na, an alcoholic; and father of 2-year-old Sun Hei

It is also difficult for compulsively dependent people to encourage independence in the toddler. The compulsively dependent parent has a great need to be needed, whether or not this overwhelms the child. The trade-off—allowing the child to be more independent and letting go of the need to be needed—may not feel worthwhile to the parent. Mee Na says:

> *This for me was the real trap of motherhood. I could always couch my feelings and decisions in terms of what was best for Sun Hei. I didn't have to decide what was best for me. I think at times I depended on Sun Hei more than that little fellow could ever have depended on me.*

And yet parents do learn how to encourage these skills of independence. Sometimes the child may learn later than other children; but most do learn if encouraged. In learning, the child attains mastery.

Remember that with any developmental benchmark there is a range of time during which it is normal for a child to learn a specific task, whether it is drinking from a cup or learning to tie his shoes. At whatever point this happens, you should appropriately encourage a task so learning can begin (Crown, 1980).

> *When I realized that it wasn't too late to encourage Monique to be independent, I felt a great relief. Maybe I hadn't screwed up her life after all.*
>
> —Jorge, a compulsive overeater and ACoA, married to Holly

Impulse Control

RULE: *Parents need to encourage children to develop control over their impulses.*

Singly, toilet training, masturbation, and aggression represent difficult issues for most parents. Yet they all begin to be issues for both parent and child during the toddler stage. Unfortunately, they all come at once. No parent has the luxury of dealing with only one of these at a time. These developmental issues are difficult for many parents because they are often related to areas that remain unresolved to some degree in the parents' own lives, particularly if drug addiction was present during their childhood.

Toilet Training

Children want to be like the adults who surround them and to master the tasks that they see the adults around them perform. Boys and girls want to go to the bathroom like they see Mommy and Daddy do. They want to get out of diapers and wear underwear like big people. They are just not sure how to go about it. To develop a sense of control, they need adult guidance and encouragement, positive guidance, clear and consistent encouragement.

This means that each child will be working on his or her own timetable, not yours. Interfering with the child's timetable can create problems. Jeon Wok recalls his own childhood dependence on his mother, who was married to a drug addict and compulsive gambler:

> I never learned to wipe myself until I started the first grade. I remember my mother saying to call her, and I would. I feel weird now thinking of how dependent I was on her and how dependent she was on me. It has taken me a longer time than most to learn to care for myself.

Masturbation

Masturbation is self-stimulation of the genitals. Both boys and girls do it, and it is normal behavior (Schor, E., 1999). When children touch their genitals in public or in the presence of the family, they are not trying to be provocative. Children do not have an adult sense of sexuality. They do not know what intercourse is. They are just touching a part of their bodies that makes them feel good, much like they suck their thumbs.

Sometimes when children touch themselves, it is a sign that something is amiss. They may be tired or bored and trying to take care of their own needs by giving themselves pleasure. Parents have discovered many ways of dealing with this, from asking the child if she is tired or hungry, to distracting her, to telling the older toddler that he can touch himself in his room but not in front of company. Jorge elaborates:

> It was difficult for me to gently and nonjudgmentally tell Monique when she was 5 that she could go to her room, but that we as a family did not touch our privates in public. Once Holly and I started to establish what our family rules were going to be, it got easier. We talked it through and realized that even though we were both impulsive, we didn't want Monique to be quite that way.

Children learn by watching the behaviors that their parents model, and they often mimic what they see. For example, if sexual activity occurs in front of a child, she will be curious. But even if she attempts to repeat what she saw, she does not know what she is doing. Because they are likely to imitate what they see, children need as much protection from adult sexuality as you can provide. As the most obvious, but also the most necessary ways of accomplishing this, we suggest that you close bedroom doors and keep the sounds that accompany sexual intercourse low.

Aggression

According to Shelov (1998), "the best way to prevent violent behavior is to give your child a stable, secure home life with firm, loving discipline and full-time supervision during the toddler and preschool years." Aggression is a difficult issue for parents to deal with, particularly within a family affected by drug addiction, because anger is so often an issue. Children learn from watching, and in homes affected by addiction, violence is often a response to anger.

Children need to learn the safe bounds of their anger. For the toddler, a loud "No!" and turning your back to your child is often sufficient. Sometimes that will not be enough, however, and you will need to set limits and enforce them. Children need consistent boundaries even if the parent feels uncomfortable setting them. "I would feel so guilty if I even yelled at Sun Hei that I would hate myself," Mee Na moans.

In a home where there is frequent verbal and physical aggression, children may act out what they see, frequently with the same person who received the abuse. For example, in a home where addiction and physical violence are present, if the mother is frequently hit, it is not uncommon for a young child to also hit his mother. The child is mimicking what he has seen, and he may be experimenting with how to deal with anger by using his mother as a safe target.

In this situation, the child needs to learn that he cannot hit his mother. A loud "No!" may be enough to get this point across. It's important in such a home for the mother not to take any of the anger she has for her husband out on her child. This does not mean that a mother in such a situation should be unresponsive and just accept her toddler's behavior. But when she disciplines her child, she should remember that he's her *child*, not her husband in her child's guise, and do so in an appropriate, nonmalicious way.

If the child is the target of verbal or physical abuse, it is vital that the abuse is stopped immediately, even if it means reporting your spouse to the authorities. If you feel that you have crossed over the line with your child, you need help. Groups like Parents Anonymous are available to support both parents, as are private therapists.

Children at this age feel that they are the center of the universe, and that all actions that surround them are a result of their actions and thoughts (Schor 1999). If possible, the abusing parent needs to apologize to the child. The child needs to receive the clear message that the abusing parent is truly sorry and loves the child, even though the parent has a problem showing this love. It is vital to reassure the child that she did not cause the uproar, and that she did not deserve the abuse.

Parenting the Preschool Child: Age 3 to 5 Years

The preschool child is now talking, probably toilet trained, and ready to set about learning another set of tasks. The next challenge for preschoolers is to learn about socializing in-groups and within the family. To do this, children need to begin to develop some understanding of how they feel. Not only do children express feelings at this age, but they also begin to recognize how and why they have certain feelings. To accomplish this, children begin by developing rudimentary concepts of right and wrong, "good" and "bad." This complements their growing understanding of their own motivation and ego development (Rosen, 1980).

The Impact of Addiction

Addiction affects the process of personality development in many ways. Many parents had unrealistic demands placed upon them as they grew up. Unfortunately, they may place similar demands upon their children because they have come to view this as normal.

The Perfectionistic Child

Parents in alcoholic and drug-addicted families often leap at any indications that their child is able to help them. They come to look at their children as little adults, much as they were seen when they were children. If the family's expectation level is too high, the child will experience repeated failure to meet his parents' expectations. This causes children to begin to internalize this constant failure, continually judging themselves by standards that are too high (Chess, Thomas, & Birch, 1976). There are two equally rigid outcomes to this extreme: either the child will become a perfectionist and constantly feel inadequate, or he will give up and stop trying because he can never measure up to his parents' unrealistic expectations. Either extreme portends problems for both the child and the family. The perfectionist child frequently becomes obsessed with performing. The child who has given up frequently becomes depressed and may later act out his frustration, or withdraw completely.

The Parental Child

The family tradition of perfectionism can be passed down from one generation to another (Papp, 1983). In the drug-addicted family, this is usually accomplished by making children into parent-figures. The child strives to be like her parent, and to do this, she believes she must do everything right. Once children are put in parental roles, they try their hardest to fulfill the perceived expectations of their family. They attempt to take care of their parents instead of having their parents take care of them. They learn that becoming part of a greater group, like the family (and ultimately, all relationships), means taking care of someone at the expense of their own needs.

Jeon Wok recalls trying to control how much his father drank:

> My heart would break seeing my father drink. Here I was age 5 and crying, telling my
> father that I didn't want him to die, and please not to drink so much. My mother later told
> me that she could hear her own words pointed back at her. Somehow I had associated
> drinking with dying. Mom said that she knew that we had some serious problems ahead,
> but she didn't know what to do about it.

And Mee Na recalls her own early childhood:

> I was the little miss, the little princess, but what this really meant was that I was an adult
> and no longer a child. I feel sometimes that my childhood ended as soon as I could walk
> and talk. My parents tell me what a cute baby I was, but after that they are vague about
> my childhood. I remember around age four trying to get their approval on whatever I did.
> I don't remember if they ever complimented me. I feel like I have been striving to get my
> "parents," in the guise of my boss or even my husband, to say I've done well. Some times
> I even put my 5-year-old, Sun Hei, in that role and hang on to his approval. I know it's
> a bit of a role reversal, but I still get stuck.

The Acting-Out Child

Even when children have given up trying to please their parents, they may still be
subtly trying to take care of them (O'Gorman & Ross, 1986). A child may take care
of his parents by either keeping out of the way or by offering himself as a problem
via his troublesome behavior. The authors have found that this is often the child's
attempt to unite the family and hence care for his parents. Some family therapists
are able to begin to discern this pattern, but such enlightenment in family therapy
is recent. Says Jeon Wok:

> I remember my family going into counseling just before I started the first grade. I wasn't
> fully toilet trained, and I couldn't stand being away from my mother. I would also break
> things, lots of things, on purpose. There was a real concern about whether or not I could
> begin first grade. Looking back on it now, I realize that I was trying to keep my father
> home and involved with my family.
>
> My mother would cry about Dad being gone, and then she would pretend that every-
> thing was all right. But I knew he was drinking. Only when I was older did I find out that
> when he was not home, he was also gambling. I knew how to get him home, and that was
> to tear up the place. Unfortunately my behavior was always the focus of therapy. We were
> in therapy off and on for years. They never dealt with Dad's drinking or gambling, or my
> attempt to parent my mom and bring my dad home. I wish there had been Gamblers
> Anonymous for my father back then. Maybe he would have joined. But he never joined
> AA, so I guess I'm just wishing it could have been different.

RULE: *Allow your child to be a child.*

As easy as it is to have a child assume an adult role, it is also possible to begin to move a child back into a child's role. Children need to know that their parents are in charge and can manage their lives. Children need to feel cared about and protected. To allow your child to be a child, start treating him or her like one. Tell them how much you love them. Remove excess responsibilities. Expect your child to act like a child and not like an adult. There is plenty of time for them to be adults later. Be aware that your children will probably react to the change by doing things the old way until they realize that this change is safe.

Guidelines for Parenting Your Toddler

- *Don't bring adult concerns to your child, no matter how mature they seem.* They shouldn't have to know that there is very little money, or that Daddy puts too much pressure on Mommy to have sex. They also should not be asked to protect one parent from another.

- *Do have child-based rituals.* Have a playtime with your child. Try to let your imagination join your child's and have fun together. If spontaneity is a problem for you, play an organized game with your child. Read your child to sleep at night. It can be just one short story. Have a nighttime ritual that is predictable—a story, a kiss, and an "I love you." It is important for your child to sleep in the security of your love. Have the day begin in a way that is predictable, for example, you and your child always having breakfast together.

- *Don't get into power battles with your toddler.* Don't just say "No" to get your point across, use short phrases to explain. It is better to let your child know that the reason why you say "No" is because it is in her best interest, and not just because you want to exert power over her by saying "No." For example, when your child wants to touch something hot, it is better to provide an explanation along with the "no." If your child insists on touching something hot, it is important to gently move her away from the threat, and hold her if she throws a tantrum.

- *Don't sleep with your child unless the circumstance is unusual,* e.g., he has a nightmare or is ill. Sleeping with your children will only teach them to depend on you unnecessarily.

- *Don't be overanxious.* If your toddler is having a temper tantrum and is safe, tell him that you'll talk about it when he calms down, and walk away.

- *Do calm down a child who is throwing a tantrum* by putting your arms around him or her and saying gently, "It is so hard to be 2 (or 3 or 4)."

- *Do give yourself a time-out if you need one.* If you feel that you are about to lose control, instead of yelling,, try sitting on the floor for a few moments until you are more calm.

- *Do guide your child toward independence.* Realize that when a child says "no," he or she is proclaiming separateness. Don't overreact.

- *Do answer any and all questions your children ask concerning sensitive topics such as sex and drug addiction.* Give short, simple, and age-appropriate responses. If they don't understand, they'll ask again. Read materials designed to help you speak to your children about these issues. The more often you answer a "difficult" question, the more practice you get in finding a way to speak with your children about awkward topics. Another reason to do this, even when it's a struggle, is that studies show that kids get information from their peers, and this information is often incorrect. So to have an informed child, and to keep your credibility as an "expert," keep talking.

- *Do be consistent.* As soon as you find something positive that works, keep using it.

- *Do keep telling your children how much you love them.* Remember to express your love in words and actions.

- *Do love yourself.* Parenting is hard work, and you need to care for yourself so that you can continue to care for your children.

Summary

Children need guidance. Growing up is hard work, and mastering developmental tasks such as emerging independence, toilet training, and impulse control may seem overwhelming and frustrating to toddlers and preschoolers at times. If a toddler or preschooler feels the need to accommodate the emotional demands of a parent who feels overwhelmed by his or her life, this may interfere with these developmental tasks and hinder his or her healthy development. It is important to let children be children.

Remember, parenting is a learned skill. You can—and in fact, without realizing it, you will—implement parenting skills at the same time as you are acquiring and developing them. Sometimes you may have to act on faith that the advice of friends, a doctor, or even something you read in a book, is valid and useful, but as you gain a little experience, you will incorporate it with exciting results. As the toddler learns independence by walking in small steps and falling down frequently, so you will learn parenting skills. Don't be afraid to take the first step. It is never too late.

CHAPTER 10

Parenting the
School-Age
Child

I really dreaded taking Audrey to school. Somehow I felt that her teachers would judge me for being fat. I felt vulnerable and I resented the school, and probably undermined their work with Audrey.

—Karl, age 30, a compulsive overeater and ACoA,
and married to Gretchen, a bulimic

When Your Child Starts School: A New Phase of Parenting

Starting school can be a traumatic time for both children and their parents. For the parent, the first day of school signifies the entrance to a new phase of parenting. While most families have some problems letting go when their children start school, creating a partnership with a school may pose a greater problem for families affected by addiction. Creating partnerships of any kind is difficult for parents affected by drug addiction, for it requires two parenting skills that may be underdeveloped: trust and the ability to negotiate. Karl's experience is typical:

All of my suspiciousness and compulsive worrying about life in general began to be focused on the school. Would Audrey have the right teacher? Would they protect her if other kids picked on her? My fears also came out. Would they judge my fatness or my wife's thinness and see us as unfit parents?

Audrey's entry into school brought up my own childhood issues about school. Through-
out my childhood, I dreaded that my teachers would find out about my father's drinking.
Was this why I was, in some ways, advertising our family's problems by being fat, to force
her teachers to help her? Of course, I also worried whether Audrey was as bright as we
thought she was. I obsessed over it all.

Kindergarten Through Grade 3: Partnering with the School

RULE: *Parents must learn to trust the school.*

Your attitude toward your children's school affects your children's adjustment to
it. If you support the school, your children will learn how to transfer trust from
one adult to another. If you question the teachers and principal, second-guessing
and undermining them, your children will be caught in the middle. They may begin to obsess about whom to believe: should they trust you, their Mommy or Daddy,
or should they believe their teachers?

The first major indication of your attitude is your ability to trust the school. Do
you withdraw? Not get involved? Or are you overinvolved? Trust is complicated.
You must trust the school to make the right decision for your child. This means
learning to share power. This doesn't mean that you are not involved. You should
be involved, but you will be giving up some of the control that you have had until
now as the primary decisionmaker for your children. This also means learning to
trust your children's emerging ability to learn and to follow through. This requires
letting them go as well.

The Impact of Addiction

Learning to trust may be especially difficult for the adult child of an addict, for it
involves giving up control and being vulnerable (Black, 1981). Trust is also a major
hurdle for the recovering person who is trying to do everything right (Wallace,
1985). Those who have been affected by drug addiction fear that they will be judged.
Marisol, an ACoA and a recovering alcoholic and drug addict, sighs:

> *That was me, particularly after the birth of my second child, Milagros, when I had a "slip."*
> *Having two children began to feel like two too many, and I began to drink. Unfortunately,*
> *it was a public slip. I even went drunk to Salazar's first parent-teacher conference. After*
> *that, I felt that I had to make it up to Salazar, and prove to the school that I was a fit parent.*
> *I decided to do this by controlling everything the school did to make sure they did it*
> *right. Eventually, I learned to take my own inventory and not the school's. I owned my*
> *perfectionism as my problem.*

The authors have found that parents who have been affected by addiction often approach the school in a guarded fashion. They either want to remove control from the school entirely or relinquish all authority to the school. Parents affected by addiction often view the school as the ultimate parent. Since many people who have lived with addiction know parents as punitive figures who can't be fully trusted, they expect the same from the school. This may lead them to either grossly over- or underreact to imagined or real events.

The answer to this dilemma is to begin to learn to trust the school. This doesn't mean suspending all your own thoughts about what is best for your child and blindly following the school's directions. It does mean entering into a partnership with the school where you don't doubt the sincerity of their motivation, but may at times question their decisions.

The Acting-Out Child: A Special Issue

Children become disobedient for many reasons. According to Dr. Edward Schor, editor of *Caring for Your School-Age Child* (American Academy of Pediatrics, 1999), "Some children, because of inherited personality traits, are more disposed to aggression. Others who are very active, strong-willed, or impulsive have more trouble learning to control their aggression."

But be aware of the behavior that you model for your child. Remember, one of the primary ways that children learn is through imitation Your behavior as a parent and spouse will help your children determine what acceptable behavior is. If you are aggressive or allow aggressive behavior between your children, they will learn that this is acceptable behavior. This is true for discipline as well.

Physical punishment is rarely, if ever, effective. Dr. Schor goes on to state that physical punishment is a sign that the parent is unable to manage his anger appropriately, and that a parent responding to a child's aggression with aggression of his own will usually only make the situation worse.

Aggressive behavior may have other causes, including split loyalties between divorced or battling parents, or between parents and the school. When a child is asked to divide her loyalty or to choose a side, she often opts instead to act out her conflict by breaking the rules. Her defiant behavior is designed to call attention to her pain and her fear about what she is being asked to do. It is almost as if the child is saying, "I'm going to make sure *you* will notice me and take care of me, because I can't do what you are expecting me to do." Marisol speaks about her son Salazar's behavior:

> Salazar began to have problems before I went back into an addiction treatment center. I really challenged the authority of the school and confused Salazar. I recall one incident

when he was learning multiplication. I taught him my way, and when he said the teacher was doing it another way, I told him the teacher was wrong. Shortly afterwards, he began to be a behavior problem in school. It was almost as if he couldn't be good since I was telling him that in essence he had to choose between loyalty to the school or to me.

The school was aware that something was wrong, and they asked me to come in for a conference. I did. Drunk. I felt that they were picking on Salazar. I left in a huff. I drove over there and took Salazar home with me afterwards. I really wasn't safe to drive. The school called Miguel at work and told him what had occurred. This led to a major blowup, one of many, with Salazar back in the middle, because "his teacher had made Mommy and Daddy fight." Poor Salazar, always taking responsibility for the problems, always his mother's protector.

Bring the teachers and administrators at the school into a partnership with you, and make them aware of the reasons for at least some of your child's acting-out behavior. If teachers and administrators are aware of what is happening at home, they can help by working with your child in school and even evaluating your child to see if she needs professional help. Even if there have been embarrassing situations in the past with your family and school personnel, it is important for the sake of your children for you to move forward and *engage the school as a partner.* People will respect your intent to help your children and will be willing to let go of past mistakes. It might help if you acknowledge past negative interactions with school personnel, and make amends. You can do this by becoming the very best parent you can be at this time and sharing with school personnel what you are doing, in general terms, to deal with your family's circumstances.

Marisol found that this worked wonders:

We were lucky that when things calmed down at home, so did Salazar. The school was very helpful in working with Salazar once they understood what was going on at home. They were also able to give him support while I was away at the treatment center.

Guidelines for Partnering with Your Child's School

In working with the school, follow these guidelines:

- *Get involved with school activities.* One way to learn to trust the school is to get to know it. Become involved in school-based activities. Volunteer for school events. You don't need to attend every single one, just enough so that you, your child, and the school know that you care enough to be involved. School trips, bake sales, book sales, and special events all provide opportunities for you to get to know the school personnel and policies. It is also an interesting way to get to know your child in a social setting. There is really no reason not to get involved. Take a personal day from work. After all, if your children aren't your personal concern, what is?

- *Go to parent-teacher conferences.* These are opportunities for you to sit down with your child's teachers, consult with them, and ask them questions. Most schools set several days, afternoons, or evenings per year exclusively for parent-teacher conferences. You can also call a parent-teacher conference yourself if you are concerned about a specific problem or about your child's progress in general.

- *Go over homework with your child.* It is important for your child's education that you support the school's efforts. While the school is the main academic educator, it can't do the job without the parents. As a concerned parent, you should also know what your child is learning and how she or he feels about it.

- *Join the parent-teacher organization.* Become an active partner, not only with the school, but also with other concerned parents. Your child's school needs your support.

- *Encourage the school to address addiction and drug abuse and support its efforts to do so.* You are now knowledgeable about how addiction affects families, children, and parents. Work with your school to address these issues in the curriculum and among the faculty.

- *Watch your own tendencies toward perfectionism and impulsivity.* Try not to act these out. Like all people, teachers and school administrators do sometimes make mistakes. If there is a problem with a teacher, don't confront the administration first. Try to work it through. Remember, you are a model for how your children will handle conflict.

Grades 4 Through 6: Working with Your Child

RULE: *Parents need to learn to monitor their child's schoolwork.*

Some parents find the task of working with their child on schoolwork an enjoyable challenge. Others have difficulty, and it is often their children who have the most trouble with school. The task of teaching your children to manage homework is an important one. For children, learning how to pace themselves, when to do an assignment, and prioritizing are important lessons, not only for school but also for life. For example, children need to learn that they won't finish an assignment due on Monday if they start it a half-hour before bedtime on Sunday night. Parents should also realize that this scenario is not a good way to prepare a child for going to sleep, as the combined pressure of homework and a short time frame can leave a child unsettled, resulting in sleeplessness. When children and parents work together, a rhythm of schoolwork can eventually be developed.

The Impact of Addiction

Drug addiction affects children's school life in numerous ways, some less obvious than others. For example, children who grow up in a home with a parent who is actively addicted to drugs or alcohol often have to hunt for a safe place to do their homework. A safe place to do homework is one that is quiet, that allows the child to concentrate, and that has room to lay out and organize his papers and work. Homes with one or more adults who are active addicts are frequently not conducive to studying. This means that the child must have an alternative place to study. The nonaddicted parent needs to help his or her child find a safe study area and encourage the child to go there. Safe places can be a library, an after-school center, or a friend's, neighbor's or relative's home. If the school is made aware of the active disease at home, teachers may be able to encourage your child to do some of his work during free time in the school day. Talk to your child's guidance counselor if there is active drug addiction at home. Trust the school to work with you on this.

The Perfectionist Child Revisited

As we stated in the previous chapter, the roots of destructive perfectionism can be planted at any time in a child's life. Perfectionism often emerges when the child begins to receive homework, however. Homework is the first concrete series of tasks that the child receives from someone outside the family. You may note warning signs of perfectionism earlier. For example, if your 4-year-old behaves in a manner that would elicit the description "perfect little miss," or "the perfect man of the house," he or she may be a budding perfectionist. Excellent, even oddly mature behavior in very young children often does not elicit the alarm in a parent or teacher that an older child's intense need for perfect grades can generate. And yet the cause for both behaviors can be the same: the child's need for perfection and for total control over his or her environment

When a child comes from a home where addiction is present, their need for perfection is often simply the need to try to control all that is controllable in a chaotic home environment. Adult children of drug addicts often create chaos around themselves. They have become so accustomed to chaos that they create it—however inadvertently—so that they have something around which to organize their responses to the world. Their children, if reared in a home organized around chaos, will learn to respond accordingly.

This was the case with Audrey when she reached fourth grade. It became apparent that the "perfect little miss" had some big problems. Recalls Karl:

> *I blamed myself. Growing up in a home with addiction, I vowed that I wouldn't marry anyone who drank. I didn't. I married someone who ate, and then purged. At first I thought it was cute that Audrey would be there to take care of me or to ask my wife Gretchen if she should call the doctor after Gretchen had just thrown up again. Now it doesn't seem so cute at all to watch her pull her hair out when she can't do a math problem correctly."*
>
> *Relief came from an unexpected source. The school turned out to be as worried as we were. They had Audrey seen by the school psychologist, who suggested we go to the Child Guidance Clinic for family counseling. It's helping, and I feel like my trust in the school has been rewarded.*

Homework Guidelines

Since homework can be a troublesome area, here are some guidelines that the authors have found useful:

- *Do homework at a set time each day.* Have a regular time of day when your child is expected to do homework. This may be directly after school before he goes out to play or right after dinner. You can experiment with what time works best for your child. Each child has his or her own needs. Some need to blow off energy after a day of sitting still in school. Others need to build on the structure of the school day to enable them to focus on their schoolwork before they play. Get to know your children individually so you can encourage them to do whatever is best. Teach your children to be consistent in their approach.

- *Go over your child's homework.* Find out which of you is the best parent to either go over your child's homework or to go over a particular subject. Share your expertise, whether it's in math, English, history, or some other subject.

- *Praise your child's work.* Reward children with praise for what they've done. Remember, there will be mistakes. This is normal. Don't be overly critical. Find something great in what your child has done—penmanship, creativity, or courage in tackling a different subject. Praise them for mastering a thorny problem, or for trying and not giving up.

- *Homework problems should be reported to the teacher.* If your child doesn't bring home schoolwork but his peers do, the teacher should be informed that somehow your child is not getting the message that there is work that needs to be done at home. Or if your child is having continued problems with mastering an aspect of math or English, consult your child's teacher.

- *If problems persist, get help from the school.* Request a consultation with the teacher, then the guidance counselor. Your child may need a special approach to learning, which may only be determined by doing evaluation testing.

- *Spend quality time with your child.* Don't let homework time be the only time you and your children sit down together. This will encourage your child to develop problems with her homework in order to keep you involved with her.

Developing Rules for School-Age Children

RULE: *Children need clear rules with consistent enforcement.*

It is extremely important for children to have consistent rules. From consistent rules, the child learns how to make choices and to deal with consequences. It is normal for children to test rules. It is also normal for children to test what the truth is—by inventing the occasional truth (lying from time to time), but also by watching other children and adults around them and catching them in either not following the rules, or in not being truthful.

Homes with active addiction are inconsistent homes. From inconsistent rules the child will learn either rigidity, as in the perfectionist child, or that rules do not count, as demonstrated by the acting-out child. Inconsistent rule-setting, such as a parent punishing a behavior when drunk and rewarding the same behavior when sober, often puts pressure on children to develop their own rules.

Surprisingly, when children make their own rules, they are almost always more punitive and more strict than an adult would be. Since they have little life experience to guide them, and since it is normal for a child to try to please, they try to fit their actions into one of two boxes: black or white, right or wrong. Without adult modeling and guidance, these extremes can become their only frame of reference. As they mature they will have difficulty in defining a middle ground. The result can be a series of failures, as the child tries, but can never quite live up to, behaving the right way all of the time. To deal with this, the child may withdraw or act out.

Learning to distinguish shades of gray among the black and white—finding a middle ground—is a skill that most people learn later in life. Those affected by drug addiction may have even greater difficulty in learning this. States Marisol,

> *I don't feel I learned gray until maybe recently. Perhaps this is why I've been so punitive with Salazar. I saw his behavior as totally wrong since he wasn't doing what I wanted him to do.*

Guidelines for Rule-Making

It is difficult for parents to develop rules objectively for their children when they had little experience with consistent rules in their own childhood. You should remember that children need to be taught to obey—and that they *want* to obey and please their parents. This experience of consciously making rules can be positive if the adult understands the child's individual temperament. In other words, is he or she easily frustrated? Afraid to try? In need of a great deal of praise? Likely to cover failure with anger or to display other reactions? Remember, children will be frustrated when they seek to master new things. New rules create new challenges for mastery. This is part of learning and accompanies all learning. To help you along, consider the following suggested guidelines. Do not rush. Take these one at a time.

- *Have regular family meetings.* Regular meetings of a family provide a way for the family to come together, plan, air concerns, and settle problems. In such meetings, everyone gets a vote and everyone gets a say, no matter how young they are.

- *Develop rules by sitting down with your children, creating rules, and discussing them.* At family meetings, have each child contribute ideas about what needs to be done, and who would be best to do it. You and your partner need to make sure that children do not overcommit themselves, or commit to doing things that they are not yet developmentally able to do. Children will more readily follow rules when they feel they have had a role in making them.

- *Post the family's rules on the refrigerator.* Everyone goes into the refrigerator. As such it can be a focal point for family activity. Post the rules there with a daily checklist. This way you can note what's been done; if the garbage has been taken out, you don't need to preach about it. Use stars or smiling face stickers to mark a job well done or a good week.

- *Set total, not partial limits.* If you tell your child that he can splash his younger sister as long as he does not get her wet, you will have guaranteed yourself a deluge of trouble. Limits should be clear and understandable. Have clear rewards and clear consequences. Negotiate this ahead of time, particularly if there have been problems with one or more of your children following through. You can give rewards for 70 to 80% compliance, with bonuses for 90 to 100%. Discuss this with your partner and children and see what is best. Rewards can be something like a half-hour more of TV on Friday night or an extra scoop of ice cream. They should never be anything that will break the family's bankroll or compromise other family activities.

- *Don't accept excuses.* This only teaches lying and the art of excuse making. If a rule is made, it should be followed. No excuses.

- *Work instead to either negotiate the rule or to help your child comply with it.* For example, if the rule is to be home at 6 P.M. for dinner and your child is late, ask him if he remembers the rule. Make sure your child knows how to tell time. See if he needs a watch. Try to understand if the problem is peer pressure not to leave a game. Work on these issues instead of accepting an excuse, which will only teach your child to be a better excuse-maker.

- *Allowances: pros and cons.* Some experts feel that if children see that their contribution is needed within the family, this is all the reward that they require. They need not and should not be paid for doing a chore needed by the family. Under this philosophy, allowances are not earned, but rather given as a division of the family earnings so that each person may take care of personal needs. Other experts feel that an allowance should be earned and tied to chores. There is no right or wrong. Again, this is an issue to be discussed with your spouse and with your children.

If the rules aren't working, ask yourself:

- Are you making too many demands at once on your child?

- Are you expecting more than your child at this age and under these circumstances can do?

- Is the discipline understood?

- Are you trying to gain compliance by force, bullying, or bribing?

- Do directions have too many explanations, making them unclear?

- Do you both agree with what is required of your child?

- Are you keeping the child's individual temperament in mind in planning your approach?

Scheduling Children's Time

RULE: *Parents need to monitor and not overschedule their children's activities.*

As parents, you want the best for your child. This often means that you are more than willing to assist your child in pursuing any latent or manifest talents. For the child who has many talents or interests, the result can be increased stress as the child runs from the school to piano, ballet, voice, karate, swimming, and track, all scheduled and chauffeured by the parent.

The Impact of Addiction

Compulsive *overscheduling* is a common occurrence in the recovering home. Before we discuss the downside of this overscheduling, understand that there is a positive side to scheduling activities for children. Structure is helpful, and scheduled activities are important. Children need child-centered activities and a child-centered home.

Families with active addiction often have difficulty being as organized as is required for a family to have many different scheduled activities. In the recovering home, the reason for frequent of overscheduling is twofold. First, the family may be trying to make up for lost time. In the active phase of drug addiction, the children were deprived of positive parental attention. Now that the parents are in recovery, they are eager to make this up to them. Also, some recovering parents tend to overschedule their children to compensate for the guilt they feel for not being home when they need to go to meetings. They get caught in a time squeeze, as Marisol illustrates:

> *After I left the drug addiction treatment center, I really needed to go to meetings, but I felt bad that I wasn't home for Salazar. Salazar also got on my nerves. It was easier to get him involved in Little League, karate, and the Cub Scouts than to spend quality time with him. And so I did.*

The Hurried Child

In adult children of drug addicts, the lost-time phenomenon is experienced as the loss of part of childhood: lost opportunities, lost time to pursue their interests, lost time to play. Karl says,

> *As a parent, I've tried to undo what my parents 'did' to me. I wanted to give my children every opportunity to explore their interests.*

Overscheduling can inadvertently send your children the message that they need to perform and excel in all that you are "encouraging" them to do. This can burden children, who are trying to please their parents, into feeling that they have to master all of these new activities. As Karl discovered,

> *Unfortunately, Audrey has to be perfect in all she does. Our therapist tells us that our expectations are too high. Audrey tries to develop her interests, but she becomes increasingly frustrated when she isn't perfect on the third try. Somehow this must be coming from us, from Gretchen and me.*

Guidelines for Scheduling

Since scheduling is difficult, even for adults, here are four guidelines that may make the task easier. Add to them as you find other strategies that work.

- *Practice is important.* Children often become disappointed and frustrated when they cannot perform a new skill well. They need to be encouraged and rewarded, not punished or threatened into practicing. Discuss your expectations for practicing a sport or a musical instrument with your child—say, a half-hour of practice per day—and post these expectations on the refrigerator. Children also need to be encouraged to build on small steps, not to expect mastery after only a couple of tries. Overwhelming expectations are a major reason why children drop out of activities.

- *Losing interest is okay.* If children learn that they can withdraw from an activity without undue parental pressure, it makes it easier for them to commit to another. This is one way they can learn their limits and their interests.

- *Children need to be paced.* They should try one skill area at a time. Once they have some success at one activity such as soccer, dance, or clarinet lessons, they can add another one and then evaluate its impact. If you add new activities in a planful manner that builds on a child's interests and free time, your child will feel in control, not overwhelmed.

- *Children need free time.* Do not overschedule your children. Overscheduling not only creates additional pressure on children to perform, but it also puts pressure on them to juggle their schedules to get to the various activities. This is unhealthy. Children learn a great deal from free playtime, and this should be part of how they spend their time.

Your Children's Friends

> **RULE:** *Parents need to be aware of who their children choose as friends.*

During the early school-age years, children begin to form friendships. As they become more independent, they choose whom they want to be friends with, start to form bonds, and begin to socialize away from parental supervision.

Children are establishing culturally appropriate gender roles during middle childhood. Therefore, most of the friends your child chooses initially will probably be of the same sex. With these friends, they will experiment with the different aspects of what their family and the greater society expect from them (Simmons & Rosenberg, 1975; Hill & Lynch, 1983).

School-age children also have a high level of fantasy, which they tend to act out. Risk-taking becomes more common as children develop their skills and independence and have the means to experiment on a larger scale with their fantasies. As cognitive abilities develop, greater learning occurs, which can lead to more creative play (Lewis, & Lewis, 1984). Children need parental guidance, but it becomes more difficult for parents to provide as children get older and become more independent and more ambivalent about direct parental involvement. See the guidelines at the end of this section for some suggestions on how to accomplish this.

The Impact of Addiction

In *Caring for Your School-Age Child,* Dr. Edward Schor asserts, "between the ages of 5 and 12, making friends is one of the most important missions of middle childhood—a social skill that will endure throughout their lives." Making friends can be difficult for children from addicted homes. In homes with active addiction, children do not often receive the encouragement they need to develop friendships.

As we have learned, alcoholic families are generally closed systems that rarely let anyone in. Children of alcoholics know that bringing other people home may expose their family secret of addiction, and to avoid embarrassment, they often isolate themselves from other children. When the family dynamics interferes with the child's ability to form friendships, the child is not only delayed in developing only a sense of self, but also in learning what to expect from others (Simmons & Rosenberg, 1975). Says Marisol,

> I wasn't able to bring friends home, so I stopped having any friends. Of course I had acquaintances. I responded to what I thought they thought about me. I walked around embarrassed and withdrawn, for I felt others "knew" my family secret. I was so locked into how they felt that I never examined how I felt. They were more important than I was. My imagined opinion of what they thought was more valid than my own. I was dependent on them, but not close to them, for I really didn't know them. I learned dependency and distance from my friends. Now my dependence and distance is present in my marriage and with my children.

Children learn from their parents, and they may pick up the same responses— here dependence and distance—and manifest them in a different manner. Marisol notes this in her son's behavior.

> I think Salazar feels the same way. I've now had more than one slip. Every time I do, it seems Salazar gets into more trouble in school. He is so angry. He has friends, but now

that he is eleven, I worry what they are doing. I fear that he's using something. He needs to be with his friends, but if all they are doing is getting high, I wonder how close they can be? I also wonder if all his behavior in school isn't designed to keep his teachers involved but not too close.

Guidelines for Supervising Friendships

- *Let your child choose his or her friends.* But get to know them. Have them to your home. Meet them. Talk to them, make meals for them, and get to know who your child wants to be with and what their values are.

- *Make your home a safe place for kids to gather.* This way you can ensure that they will be supervised, and that you will be informed of any developing conflict.

- *Get to know your children's friend's parents.* This will be helpful when you need to follow up on where your children are and what they are doing. You may also find it enjoyable to support your child's friendships by getting acquainted with their friends' parents and doing some family activities together.

- *Know where your children are.* You must keep track of where your children are and what they are doing. Drug and alcohol use is not uncommon in the upper elementary school grades.

Summary

When children enter school, there are suddenly many more variables to deal with. Parents need to learn to work in partnership and negotiate with the school. This raises issues of trust and vulnerability for those who have been affected by addiction. In addition, parents face new challenges as children get older and their needs change. Children require active involvement from their parents in a variety of new activities, from homework to free-time activities to spending time with their friends. Active parenting means learning to be supportive and involved while learning to let go—in other words, being there, being available, and being aware, *without* being compulsive in your worrying, control, or scheduling of your child's life and time.

CHAPTER 11

Parenting the
Adolescent

Eddie is quite a handful at 15. He's reached puberty, discovered girls, and I think he's using something. He's so different from Tallie. You'd hardly know that she's there. Eddie has always made his presence felt.

—Barbara, 43, an adult child of a drug addict, and an addict herself

Adolescence is a time of major transition between childhood and adulthood. This is when children change from being just children into looking and acting, at least at times, more like adults. Adolescence is a difficult time, and young adults are often both frightened and excited at the same time and don't know what to do with their feelings. This can make them moody, angry, and self-righteous, yet also vulnerable. For all their drama, adolescents are covering up their fear of the massive physical changes going on within their bodies and the major social changes going on in their lives. They are striving to become independent, to find out who they are and what they need. To accomplish the developmental task of becoming independent, adolescents need to develop new coping methods and new support systems outside of the family.

Like any change, these new coping methods, new friends, and new ways of handling conflict and hurt will take practice for your teenage children to decide what is working as part of their new style and what should be discarded and replaced with something better. But these new coping methods, along with the increased emotions of adolescence, often result in an increase in the amount of tension and potential conflict within families.

Change is difficult. As with any period of change, expectations are in flux in families with adolescents. This is another reason why adolescence is also a period of conflict between parent and child: previously predictable patterns of family interactions are altered. Parents often alternately expect too much or too little from their adolescent children. The shifting ground causes the children to either feel like they are being treated like babies or that too much is expected from them. Both teens and their parents tend react to these changes by locking horns.

Parents find their children's adolescence difficult because they are being asked to give up the protection that they have, up until now, afforded their children. It is not easy for any parent to allow their child to go out into the world knowing that the child will be hurt. Seeing their children in pain and not being able to reach them often incites even the calmest parents to lose control. Adolescents, caught between wanting to be protected and needing to prove their independence, are often pushed by their parents' increased demands and frustration into displaying a new level of apathy. This occurs even in previously positive parent-child relationships. Yet for all the problems that occur during this period, for most adolescents this transformation into independent adults cannot happen quickly enough. And for most parents it occurs too rapidly.

Your Own Adolescence Versus Your Teen's

RULE: *Parents need to separate their own adolescence from what their children are experiencing.*

Memories of your own adolescence are sure to engender strong feelings. Often, even if you cannot recall memories before adolescence, you can remember at least part of your teenage years. The tasks of adolescence, such as separation from family and creating one's own identity, are very complex; in fact, many adults have not fully completed these tasks. As a result, the intense feelings that accompanied these issues, such as anger at authority, are often near the surface. For this reason, some adults have trouble realizing that they are no longer adolescents, and that life for their children holds more options—opportunities as well as dangers—than it did when they were in their teens.

Yet your memories of your own adolescence, however painful they may be, can help you understand your adolescent child. Besides allowing you to empathize with the turmoil your child is experiencing, clear recall of your own teen years may also help you predict what your child's next potential crisis will be. In recalling your own attempts to deal with such problems such as being rebuffed by the girl of your dreams, or not developing breasts at the same rate that every other girl did, you can help guide your children through these extraordinarily painful, yet normal, events of adolescence.

The Impact of Addiction

Being able to separate your own experiences from your teenage child's is difficult enough, but if you are still dealing emotionally with the struggles of your own adolescence, it becomes a real challenge. This is frequently the situation that the recovering parent faces. Many people who develop drug addiction began drinking in their teens. At the point when they approached dependence on alcohol, they also stopped growing emotionally (Strauss, 1976). Because the parent in early recovery may still be resolving developmental issues left over from his or her own adolescence, this makes raising a child even harder.

For the adult child of an addict, growth may have been stunted even earlier (O'Gorman, 1975). Parenting a child who is ahead of you developmentally is extremely challenging. Separating your identity from your child's and helping your teenage child go through something that you have not completed yourself can raise both your anxiety level and your child's. Children may become more anxious if they feel they are unraveling the dilemma of adolescence for both of you. They may decide that you are no better at coping with their problems than they are, in which case they'll either discount you or feel the need to rescue you. It does not feel good to fail your children, and your fear of your perceived and real limitations may make you even more anxious.

The Benefits of Alateen

What can you do? As someone who has been affected by the drug addiction of a parent or spouse, you have many resources at your disposal. One of the most useful is Alateen. Alateen is a self-help recovery program for young people who have been affected by drug addiction. It is sponsored by Al-Anon and open to teens regardless of whom the drug addict in their life is—you, a grandparent, uncle, or even a close family friend. Alateen is peer support and peer learning at its best.

Encouraging your children to go to Alateen can be extremely helpful. They will not only learn about how drug addiction has affected them, they'll also learn to take responsibility for their own thoughts and actions. By encouraging attendance at Alateen, you are also encouraging your child to learn to be independent (O'Gorman, 1984).

Alateen also has many secondary benefits. By encouraging members share their feelings, Alateen breaks down the isolation that your child may be experiencing and teaches him or her to interact in a positive, structured, peer-learning experience. Although there is an adult sponsor from Al-Anon at the meeting, the leadership of the group rotates between the teenage members. As a result, adolescents also learn other important skills: how to lead a meeting, share feelings and maybe most importantly, how to trust.

You Need to Be a Parent, Not a Peer

Unfortunately, some parents deal with the problem of being in a similar position as their child developmentally by identifying too closely with the child. They take vicarious, and perhaps unconscious, pleasure in their adolescent's acting out, with the result of spurring them on. They enjoy the attention their adolescent receives, and unconsciously incite their teenager to get more. They excuse excessive behavior as "sowing wild oats," which can foster greater excesses.

Parents in this situation see all that their teenager does as a reflection of themselves. They have not been able to conceive of their teenager as a separate person. Such parents are not parenting their teenager, but merely being a peer to their child. So who will parent a child if their parent cannot do it? Today, the answer is often the adolescent's peer group.

Another problem for children of addicts is the existence of "drinking pacts" between alcoholic fathers and substance-abusing sons. In such families, the addicts in each generation tacitly support one another's substance abuse. Often, the son's substance abuse focuses the family's attention on himself, which allows the father to maintain his authority and parental role and also keeps the family from scrutinizing the father's drinking. If your family is to become healthy, it is important that you bring such unspoken "pacts" to the surface and end them.

Eating Disorders

Researchers do not know for certain what causes eating disorders. We do know, however, that children with eating disorders are frequently depressed, with poor self-esteem, feelings of inadequacy, and stress and trauma in their lives (Schor, 1999). Family dynamics often provide the breeding ground for the development of food-related compulsive dependencies like bulimia, anorexia nervosa, and overeating. Eating disorders are more typically found in families in which there is a pressure to be thin, a particular emphasis on food, isolation, poor conflict resolution, rigidity, and overprotectiveness (Striegel-Moore, Silberstein, & Rodin, 1986). These families are actually much like a family with drug addiction, organized around food instead of a substance. This may account for the greater prevalence, reported by a growing number of clinicians, of eating disorders in adult children of addicts.

Such family dynamics are compounded by society. For families that have been unable to model control, either in the consumption of food or alcohol use, society offers a simple method to the adolescent who wants to appear to be in control: dieting. Dieting or purging can easily dovetail with the adolescent's desire to prove her maturity, control, and independence from her family, particularly if she views her family as being out of control (Steele, 1980). It can also be a way for adolescents to separate from their families and is perceived as positive by many adolescents who engage in this behavior.

Extreme dieting can also be a sign that the pressure of adolescence is too great. It can reflect a desire to return to a prepubescent appearance, maintaining oneself as a child in the eyes of society (Selvini-Palazzoli, 1978). For the child of an addict, this issue becomes even more complex. The adolescent who is dieting or purging often wishes to return to a less complex or safer time when she did not have to deal with her awakening sexuality.

Why would anyone do this to herself? Personal dissatisfaction with one part of a child's functioning can lead to an overall devaluation of herself. The child diets and purges based on positive motivation, to feel in control, and to improve her image of herself.

Becky is the daughter of two adult children of drug addicts, Catharine and Lionnel, both of whom have eating disorders (Catharine is a bulimic, and Lionnel is a compulsive overeater). From the time she was a child, Becky was concerned about her mother and father's health. She was aware that her mother's purging was not normal, and would often ask if she could call the doctor. She was equally obsessed with her father's obesity. She became a perfectionistic, parental child who was very dependent on her parents, especially her mother, Catharine. When she was in grade school, family therapy addressed Becky's obsessive perfectionism, but not her dependency. As an adolescent, she continued to be dependent on her mother and to take responsibility for caring for her mother.

When she reached puberty, Becky emulated the behavior of both parents, both of whom prized thinness, and developed an eating disorder. Becky became alarmed by the normal increase in body fat that accompanies puberty. Her insecurity led her to become increasingly sensitive to what she perceived as social demands and appropriate sex-role behavior. She longed for the prepubescent body, which is held in such high esteem in the teen fashion world. She feared that she would not be popular now that she was "fat." She felt out of control. For all these reasons she began to diet and to do what she saw her mother doing. She began to purge herself of food.

Becky wanted to improve her self-esteem. She was trying not to devalue herself, so she tried to take care of her problem in the very best way she could. Overly dependent on her mother and very loyal to her family traditions, she did exactly what she had learned from her parents in this situation. When Catharine saw what was happening to her daughter, it was too much for her: "It was like looking in the mirror for the first time," she said. "I couldn't believe what I saw."

What You Can Do for a Child with an Eating Disorder

In *Caring for Your School-Aged Child* (1999), Dr. Edward Schor states, "Anorexia nervosa and bulimia are difficult for professionals to treat; for parents they are virtually impossible to manage alone. Pleading with or punishing your child is not going to change her behavior. Even with the most sophisticated care, cures are difficult and relapses are common "

There is no single way to treat an eating disorder. Therapy, nutrition education, and medication are all components of treating an eating disorder, and a child with a very serious eating disorder may even require for residential treatment. You need to get help for yourself and your child from a professional. You also can take an adolescent child to Overeaters Anonymous, as Catharine did during her purposeful effort to curb her own eating disorder and Becky's.

> *I realized that I couldn't live through Becky anymore. I began to work my Al-Anon and Overeaters Anonymous programs, and practiced detaching with love. Eventually it worked, but it was so difficult. I used, or manipulated, if you will, the fact that Becky was very dependent on me and invited her to go to Overeaters Anonymous meetings with me. I worked on my program and began to stop purging. Becky began to change her eating behavior as well. It was scary when I realized just how much power I really had over her, but in this case, I was glad I did.*

Sexual Feelings

RULE: *Parents need to accept that their children have sexual feelings.*

Many teachers have commented that seventh grade is the worst grade to teach. Everyone is in some phase of puberty and they all want to touch each other, but they don't know how. So they punch, slap, and take things from each other all day long.

Sexual feelings begin to stir prior to puberty. Girls and boys begin to notice each other. They begin to take greater interest in their appearance, they become flirtatious. And then they begin to change physically. The age at which puberty occurs varies between boys and girls, with girls tending to mature earlier. The actual age of the onset of puberty is becoming earlier, meaning that for some precocious children early adolescence does not begin in junior high school but in elementary school (Bell, 1980).

Whenever puberty occurs, parents find it difficult to accept that their children are having sexual feelings. In some ways, dealing with their children's emerging sexuality is the most difficult problem that parents face. The greater fear is that since children have these feelings, they will act on them. This brings with it the fear that their children will fall in love and be hurt, the fear of pregnancy, and the fear of sexually transmitted diseases. And there is reason for concern: many adolescents are becoming sexually active at younger ages. This is complicated by the AIDS epidemic, which can add a fatal element to adolescent sex. Parents may also have strong feelings and beliefs about the morality of adolescent sex.

It is necessary to be clear with your children regarding your family's values about sexuality. But remember to always be open to discussion with your children, even if the topic is very uncomfortable. The more you speak about it, the easier it will become. Use prompts that exist readily in your life. For example, speak about movies, or TV shows, or stories in the news and use these to launch into a conversation that will convey your feelings and provide an opportunity for your child to express his or her views. This is when real education and dialogue can occur.

The Impact of Addiction

Drug addiction loosens emotional boundaries within families, which can lead to an increase in the level of sexual tension (Steinglass et al., 1993). In some families, this can foster a type of intense emotional closeness where children bond with a parent and begin to parent their parent. In the process, they may reject the efforts made by the same sex parent to care for the opposite-sex parent, perceiving their same-sex parent as incompetent to meet the needs of their opposite-sex parent. In all innocence, the child feels that only he or she can step into the breach.

Intoxication can create confusion as to who is who within a family. It is not uncommon for a father who is intoxicated to call his daughter by his wife's name, or to even think that his daughter is his wife. This can lead to inappropriate touching, fondling, name-calling, or even physical acts. The potential for sexual closeness between parent and child is not limited to the drinking parent. The child's need to comfort the nonaddicted parent through such activities as getting into bed with their parent when the addicted parent is out of the home can lead to the same type of inappropriate activity. Sadly, incest occurs with much greater frequency in homes where active addiction is present (Black, 1985).

It is no wonder that those affected by drug addiction have difficulty dealing with their children's sexuality. To deal successfully with these issues, a parent must have resolved the problems from his or her own childhood—and resolving your own issues while parenting an adolescent is a great deal of pressure. Catharine, who is also an ACoA, recalls some of her adolescent memories:

> I remember that when I was a teenager, I had to be careful what I wore, because my father would stare at my body. For example, I would never walk around in a nightgown. I always wore a bathrobe, no matter what the temperature was. I was most afraid that he would do something when he was drunk. So it's hard for me to see Becky, who is just reaching puberty, walking around in front of Lionnel. I feel I need to protect her. I know it's crazy—Lionnel would never do anything to her—but my fear is still there.

It is important that these childhood issues to be dealt with. If there was any incest or fear of incest in your family of origin, you will need therapy along with—not in lieu of—your 12-step program, to help you resolve this. And these issues can be resolved if you pick a good therapist to work with. Remember, as difficult as these problems are to confront, it is better to resolve them within yourself than to pass them on to another generation.

Substance Abuse and Adolescents

RULE: *Parents need to talk to their children about alcohol and drug use and intervene early if they even* suspect *alcohol or drug abuse.*

Many children begin to experiment with alcohol and drugs in middle or junior high school. Others begin in elementary school. Like the sexual experimentation it often accompanies, the use of mood-altering substances is usually hidden from parents. Parents may only begin to realize that their child has a problem when he or she is older. Unfortunately, by then the signs of a developing problem are often too difficult to miss (Finn & O'Gorman, 1981).

Guilt, Guilt, Guilt

Guilt is an extremely strong emotion, not only for the drug addict, but also for other family members (Wallace, 1985). Guilt is what stops many families with drug addiction and/or other addictions from dealing with their children's substance abuse. This guilt can be paralyzing, leading to intense denial until the evidence of a child's addiction is overwhelming. Guilt can inadvertently precipitate adolescents' alcohol or drug use, and it can also deter parents from talking to their children, leaving them to struggle with their peers' use of alcohol and drugs. Barbara had known since Eddie was about 12 that he was using drugs.

> I knew, but I didn't want to know. I was so wrapped up in my own guilt that yet another generation was experiencing addiction, and that I hadn't been able to stop it, that I just couldn't deal with Eddie. I devoted myself to my newly won recovery, hoping that somehow this would help Eddie. Of course it would have helped if I had spoken to him, but I was immobilized and I couldn't. Dealing with him began to feel like a distraction from what I needed to do for myself, so I just didn't deal with him. I felt so guilty, so sorry for myself, that I began drinking and using again. It was only when Eddie announced that he was going to drop out of high school that I realized I had to get involved. Peter and I knew the reason, and it was drugs. When we finally confronted Eddie, I knew why we had avoided it for so long. He told us, "You have your drug—booze—and I have mine. What's the big deal?

Her husband, Peter, tells the story from his perspective:

> I've been very supportive to Barbara since she began her battle with booze and pills. I know it was tough, the slips back into using alcohol she had. But I vowed I wouldn't leave her. I guess you can say I'm loyal, one of my better traits.
>
> When Eddie became so obviously ill, I realized that I had to take some firm action. I just couldn't focus on Barbara to the exclusion of the kids. Her drinking, at the point that Eddie became ill, made me feel that I had to choose between them. I did. I put energy into Eddie, maybe for the first time in his life. Barbara, no longer the sole focus of my attention, actually began going back to AA. I went to more Al-Anon meetings. Together, we confronted Eddie.

Families in recovery tend to take on too much responsibility for their children's drug and alcohol problems (Wallace, 1985). Despite the fact that parents do this out of love, this does not help the child. When a family takes on too much responsibility, they deny their child the opportunity to face his own behavior. This only delays the child in dealing with his problem and may actually increase the likelihood of further substance use. This is what happened to Eddie. Says Barbara,

> Peter and I were so filled with guilt that we had to deal with it. So we took care of our guilt, and ourselves, first. I had a slip. We eventually got around to trying to figure out what to do with Eddie. By then, the message Eddie had from us was that he wasn't to blame for his actions. So he blamed us, and initially, we took that blame. We believed we couldn't do anything right at that point. Thank goodness we just took him and ourselves to an addiction treatment center, and I started AA. We stopped trying to take care of Eddie in isolation.

Barbara discusses another reaction of some recovering families to their children's substance abuse.

> At least I'm not as bad as some parents I meet in AA. At the first sign of any use they cart their kids off to a meeting. I think that meetings must be the only time that they spend with their children. I know kids drink early, but a 12-year-old at AA because he had a couple of beers? Come on! I wonder if some of these parents don't in some ways encourage their kids to use so that they can go to meetings together.

You don't need to be addicted to talk to your child about alcohol and drugs. You do need to do some homework. Consider your values, your behaviors, your personal and family history, your recreational patterns and entertaining practices. Once you have had an honest talk with yourself and your spouse, then you're ready to speak to your child.

The Child's View of Substance Use

Children of addicts often have an extreme reaction to their peers' alcohol and drug use. The authors have typically found that young children of alcoholics' reactions fall into one of three categories.

- *Some will find peers who are experimenting early, and they will join them.* So great is their fear that they will also develop a problem with alcohol or drugs that these children can't wait to find out what will happen to them. So they start using early. If they do not immediately develop the same problems that they see in their parents, they believe they are home free. Of course, children who are just beginning to experiment with substance abuse will not immediately develop the same problems with alcohol or drugs that their parents have. That takes time. But they *can* develop harmful patterns of abuse, and even addictions in adolescence. Unless there is someone present in their lives who understands this difference, adolescent children of addicts will feel that they have escaped developing an addiction.

- *Others will use drugs, but not the same ones as their parents.* Like Eddie, they rationalize this as having a personal drug of choice. They feels that this is understandable and justified as long as they do not use the same substance that has caused demonstrated negative effects in their family.

- *Still other adolescents will refrain from any alcohol and drug usage.* They will also have immediate negative reactions to their peers and friends who use alcohol and drugs. They will experience feelings of betrayal, anger, and possible depression over their friends' use. They may experiment with alcohol or drug use, but it will be much later than their peer group, when they are older and surer of themselves.

Enlightened parents realize that their child's feelings about alcohol and drug use is, in part, a reaction to unresolved family issues. While this is an important realization, it is even more important to break through the conspiracy of silence that can exist within a family and begin a *dialogue* with your children about alcohol and drug abuse.

This does not mean just telling them your story. It means getting to know your children and letting them know their family history (who else in the family has a drug or alcohol problem) and its impact on their lives and that of their children. To have this conversation, you must ask your children what they are doing and what their friends are doing in terms of experimentation with substances. It also means finding out how they feel. Of course, you can't sit down, have one conversation, and acquit yourself. This has to be part of an ongoing dialogue.

Family Messages and Expectations About Teen Alcohol Use

If addictions run in your family, the safest message to send your children about alcohol use is not to drink. By not drinking, your children will cut the risk of developing an addiction to zero percent. Unfortunately, this is also the most difficult message for most children to hear and accept.

Adolescents experiment with alcohol for a variety of reasons: because they have seen their parents and other relatives drink, because their peers drink, because they see a lack of negative consequences in the way alcohol use is glamorized in the media. Adolescents feel immortal. If they see a movie or television star engage in high-speed driving after drinking, it only serves to support the notion that people can drink without expecting physical or legal consequences. Inconsistent laws, such as those that permit the selling of drug paraphernalia, yet punish those who use drugs, compound the problem. Young people are quick to seize upon hypocrisy and will use it to defend drug use. For the same reason, many young people do not take the laws against purchasing alcohol and drinking and driving seriously; these laws are enforced inconsistently. Finally, many young people—and some medical practitioners—do not believe that children can develop drug addictions. This is not true. Young people do develop addictions, and children of drug addicts are the single most at-risk group (O'Gorman & Lacks, 1979).

This is why it is important that you are very clear about what you expect from your children in terms of alcohol and drug use. You and your spouse must make family rules and enforce them consistently. This requires parents to face the controversial issue of whether those affected by addiction should drink, even socially.

Some parents hesitate to deal with these issues, fearing that they will overreact, but it's important that your expectations for your children's behavior are clear. First, realize that your decisions about alcohol or drug use are based on your experiences and on your family's values and behaviors. Second, understand that a given behavior may have one meaning for you, and the same behavior for your child may have a very different meaning.

For example, if your family drinks wine and allows children to drink it, even in a diluted form at Passover or Christmas, your child may well consider himself to be a drinker. Given how much our society glamorizes alcohol use, the ritual or special occasion of which the wine is a part may be overshadowed in your child's eyes by the fact that he or she has had a drink. It is important that you clarify for your child the circumstances under which alcohol is used or not used in your family, by whom, and why.

If either you or your spouse abstains from alcohol, your children should know why, and if you do not think that they should drink, they should also know that, and why. If you do not drink alcohol because you are an alcoholic, but your spouse does use alcohol, clarify this to your child. Remember, your children will be watching you and waiting to know why you do what you do. They will also learn by imitating you.

Know the Law

Regardless of the expectations you set regarding your own use of alcohol and that of your children, you must be aware of the laws concerning alcohol use by minors, and you must ensure that your children understand them. Throughout the U.S., the minimum age to purchase and consume alcohol is 21, but other laws regarding minors and alcohol use vary by state. In many states, the law not only forbids the sale of alcohol to those who are underage, but also it holds servers in social settings liable for the actions of minors under the influence. This means, for example, that if you serve your daughter's boyfriend, or if you allow your daughter to serve him, you could be liable for his actions.

Setting and enforcing expectations for your adolescents around alcohol use can be complicated. Take your time, consider the nuances of your own behavior and your spouse's, and be sure to be consistent. If you are still confused, see what guidance your child's school can offer. Get more information from groups with a variety of viewpoints. Three excellent resources on this issue are The National Federation of Parents for Drug-Free Youth, Tough Love, and National Families in Action.

Be an *alert* parent and watch for the signs of alcohol or drug use. If your child or any of their friends are showing any of the following signs, get involved, talk to your children, and find out if they or their friends are using. If their friends are using, it's probably just a matter of time before your children become curious and experiment as well.

Signs of Alcohol and Drug Use in Adolescents
Health

- Frequent, excessive coughing

- Frequent infections

- Frequent small burns

- Weight loss, decreased appetite

- Weight gain, brief periods of voracious appetite (munchies)

- Frequent headaches

- Cessation of menstruation

- Hyperactivity

- Illness in the morning, throwing up, lethargy, headaches

Physical

- Bloodshot eyes

- Runny or irritated nose

- Smell of marijuana or alcohol on clothing or on breath

- Brownish-yellowish discoloration of the skin on forefinger and thumb

- Needle marks on arms or legs

- Accidents of any kind

- Dilated pupils

- Slurred, slow speech

Social and Emotional

- Change in friends to those who are known users

- Concern of friends or boyfriend/girlfriend regarding use

- Drop in grades

- Inability to think clearly

- Diminished alertness

- Excessive sleeping, decrease in energy

- Unusual mood changes, depression, or wide mood swings

- Increased anxiety

- Hallucinations or paranoia

- Sudden secretive behavior

- Change in finances—a constant need for money or an abundance of money from unexplained sources

If your child (or his friends) display several of these symptoms, talk to him about it. Then consult your family physician, mental health professional, substance abuse rehabilitation professional, or a trained member of the clergy about your next step.

The Adolescent's Need for Independence

RULE: *Parents need to encourage independence in their adolescents.*

The main task of adolescence is separation and individuation from the family (Erikson, 1963), also called growing up. The close attachment that adolescents form with their peer groups is important in completing this task. Your child's friends actually help her learn to rely less on you, her family. Peer groups also fill other roles for teens. For example, peers provide a place to obtain information and support. Adolescents often goes their friends first when they have problems, and they usually consider the advice that their peers give very carefully. For teens, peers become the new experts in resolving life's issues, and they often come to view their parents as less informed or less sensitive than their friends. Adolescents' friends and the activities they do together also provide them with a place to socialize, which teaches them independent social skills.

All this reliance on peers can belie the fact that adolescents tend to be highly ambivalent about becoming adults. To make the shift from relying primarily on their families to relying more on their friends—in other words, to achieve emotional independence from their families—adolescents actually require considerable support from their families. Parents need to guide their children in determining who is a friend and why. They need to be available with support for their children through this sorting-out phase of what teens need from friends and what they are willing to give in return. Most importantly, parents need to remember the friendships made during adolescence are subject to rapid and painful changes. Parents need to help their children realize that the bumps they encounter during adolescence can be powerful building blocks in their development of resilience, the skills necessary to deal with adversity (O'Gorman, 1994).

The Impact of Addiction

Separating yourself emotionally from your family when you feel that you are only one holding it together is a very difficult task. For this reason, many adolescents whose families are affected by drug addiction do not separate successfully (Steinglass & Robertson, 1983). Often, they lack the skills to have close friends. Many have been so involved with their families that they haven't devoted the necessary energy to learn how to develop friendships. When they do begin to separate from their families, these teens may develop dependent relationships with their peers, for they have never learned other types of relationships. In such friendships, teens may to become the caretaker, the responsible one (Black, 1979). They may choose friends who need constant care and who cannot accept responsibility for their own actions. Or they may act out, manifesting their dependency on their families in a different way (O'Gorman & Ross, 1986, Weiner, 1980). Both types are equally dependent.

Learned Helplessness

When Becky reached 16, it became apparent to Catharine that she was living through her daughter, just as her mother had lived through her. Yes, she enjoyed shopping with her, but she encouraged Becky to buy the skimpiest of bathing suits. She was as obsessed with her daughter's weight as she was with her own. She wanted to make sure that she only went out with the "right" boys, and she was careful to see that Becky didn't go steady as it was important to "play the field." When, through her 12-step program, Catharine realized that this was not a healthy relationship for either of them, she decided to break with the family tradition of mothers living through their daughters, and she withdrew.

When her mother detached, Becky panicked. With few social skills, and not having resolved her dependency needs, Becky felt abandoned. Her socializing from the time she was a preschooler had revolved around taking care of others. The two were synonymous to her. So Becky found someone else to save, someone she could also rely on to tell her what to do. The captain of the debate team became her new cause. He was a strong-willed, somewhat isolated young man. Becky was drawn to him. She felt that he needed her, and she began to take care of him. Her major decisions revolved around him. Becky's dependency had just switched its target.

Catharine, aware that this was a continuation of Becky's relationship pattern with her, intervened. She made Becky aware that this was not a healthy relationship. Eventually, Becky began to see her mother's viewpoint. After many heartrending discussions with her mother, and in the face of increased demands by her boyfriend, she broke off the relationship. In the process, she and her mother developed a healthier relationship, which included more respect for each other's differences.

By detaching, Catharine in essence had told Becky to live her own life, but hadn't prepared her daughter to do this. Becky had to face the fact that she didn't know how to make decisions for herself. Of course, she did know how to take care of others. She immediately found a substitute for her mother. When this didn't work, she needed an alternative, and Overeaters Anonymous provided the best support for her. Through the OA program, she learned to rely on herself and to make her own decisions.

Acting Out

Acting-out behavior in adolescents is frequently misunderstood. While such behavior can have many roots, it is often results from depression. An outward sullenness and an "I don't care" attitude mask anger turned inward. The adolescent may be filled with self-loathing and be acting out as a way of getting punished (O'Gorman & Ross, 1986; Weiner, 1980).

Acting-out adolescents deal with independence by stating that "it's no big deal." They withdraw from their families overtly, but they manifest a high level of problems, which keep their families involved and close, albeit negatively. This is an expression of their fear and ambivalence about being on their own in the real world. Rather than admit to feeling afraid, or acknowledge their dependence upon their parents/caregivers, these teens choose to flout rules and be "angry." They can then safely rebel against their family, society, and the world, knowing that if they keep acting out they never need worry about being alone, because the people in their lives will never trust them (Weiner, 1980).

Eddie acted out, not only getting heavily into drugs, but also by getting his girlfriend pregnant, as his mother relates:

> To Eddie, having a baby was no big deal. He was going to marry Latisha and continue high school. He was in his junior year, as was Latisha. They didn't believe in abortion and having their baby adopted and "raised by strangers" was out of the question.
>
> "Who's going to care for the baby?" we asked. "We thought you and Dad would," Eddie told us. "It will just be until we get out of school, just about a year and a half." The crazy thing is that we considered it. Peter and I figured out that I could quit my job, and he could get a second job.
>
> It took Tallie, our 14-year-old, fade-into-the-woodwork child, to ask if we wanted to do this. Peter and I, both being adult children of drug addicts, knew we could do almost anything. The question was, did we want to? This was much more difficult for us to answer. We had to stop being dependent on Eddie's need for us and ask what was good for us and what would really be helpful to Eddie. We decided that we didn't want to parent an infant again, and that if we did it anyway, we would again be giving Eddie a mixed message.
>
> When we told Eddie, it was a major blow to him. Somehow he felt that we would always be there to bail him out. The best thing we ever did for him was to say "no" and mean it. Eddie began to have to grow up.

RULE: *Let go, but be structured*

It is so difficult to let go. Your children are precious to you. You know what pain is, because you have experienced so much of it. Often, to compensate, you try to hold your children closer. This isn't good for you or your children. How can you let go, yet still give your children the love and support they need?

- *Respect the choices that your child makes.* Remember that you can guide and influence your child's choices, but you can't control them.

- *Allow adolescents to feel the real-life consequences of their actions.* Don't try to shield them from everything.

- *Talk to your kids.* Keep the lines of communication open, even if you have to initiate discussion and you don't want to. Don't let your kids' resistance to talking to you stop you.

- *Don't be blind to emerging problems.* If you think your child has a problem with drug or alcohol use, confront her. If you feel his sexual behavior is irresponsible, speak to him about it.

- *Have clear rules with rewards and consequences.* Don't accept excuses. Put your energy into refining the rules, rather than teaching your child to be a better excuse-maker.

- *Use your 12-step program.* Remember, it is a program for life.

Summary

For those recovering from the varied effects of addiction, parenting teenagers is even tougher than it is for most parents. Sometimes, developmentally, there is not much difference between parents and children, as both may be dealing with the issues of individuation and separation. Parenting a teenager means that you have to grow, sometimes just to keep one step ahead of your child and not treat your teen as an outgrowth of yourself. The issues raised earlier bear repeating here: consistency is important, as is communicating with your adolescents. The most important thing is for you to be the adult in the family. Your children need this, and you may even find it enjoyable. Remember, if you won't parent your child, who will?

CHAPTER 12

When to Seek
Professional Help

I kept working my program, but I still couldn't stop hitting my kids. I was grateful when a fellow Al-Anon member suggested that I get professional help

—Joan, age 52, an ACoA, and married to Paul, an active drug addict

What Is Professional Help?

Seeking professional help means going to a degreed professional for special assistance, or counseling. A degreed professional has received special training in medicine or mental health—including psychology, social work, or psychiatry—and drug addiction. Counselors may have many other specialties, including learning disabilities and eating disorders. Professionals are qualified to render specific services because they have received special training. Unless a person is trained and licensed, they cannot legally render a service, and they are not qualified to do so.

The Difference Between Professional Help and Self-Help

Self-help programs are peer-led groups with rotating leadership, and no designated leaders. The emphasis in these groups is on each person sharing his own experience. There is a minimum of group interaction, as the purpose of the group is to learn by hearing from one's peers, as opposed to learning by recreating in the group the same dynamics that are causing problems in your life. Isolation is decreased through such sharing, and a new perspective is learned.

Professionals are trained *not* to share their personal experience. With a professional there is an emphasis on maintaining objectivity. That can be very helpful in having one reflect and own up to responsibility for one's thoughts and actions. Professionals are also trained to intervene in a problem. In professionally run groups, confrontations are encouraged and analyzed for the important personal information they contain. Self-help programs have been found to work very well with those who are also involved in professional counseling.

Who Needs Professional Help?

Not everyone who has drug addiction or is the child or the spouse of a drug addict needs professional help. (Anthony, 1974; Russel, Strasburger, Welte, & Blume, 1983). Many of the problems that result from drug addiction can be dealt with in 12-step recovery programs and through a development of one's spiritual side. Some special problems require professional help, however. If you or a family member currently has or has had any of the specific problems listed below, a professional consultation with a mental health specialist, a doctor, or a professional member of the clergy is a good idea.

For Adults:

Mental Health

- incest

- rape

- emotional problems, such as depression or anxiety

- uncontrollable temper

- marital conflicts

Health

- recurrent headaches

- recurrent stomachaches

- any recurrent body aches or pains

- addictive diseases and disorders, including drug addiction

- compulsive overeating or other compulsive behavior

- gambling

For Children:

Mental Health

- incest or sexual abuse
- difficulty in managing temper, resulting in problems with peers or authority figures
- stealing
- depression
- high anxiety
- undue shyness
- child abuse
- child neglect
- traumatic injuries

Health

- fetal alcohol syndrome
- alcohol-related birth defects
- hyperactivity
- failure to thrive and grow
- frequent headaches and stomachaches
- any recurrent physical problem
- alcohol or drug dependence

Learning Disabilities

- difficulty in learning to read that is placing your child two or more years behind her peers
- difficulty in mathematics, such as number rotation, that is placing your child approximately two years behind her peers
- difficulty in paying attention in school, being easily distracted, or having a short attention span

Spiritual Problems in Adults and Children

Do you:

- need to understand God in your life?

- need to reconnect with God in a more formal way?

- need to be forgiven by God for one's actions?

- need to experience God's love in your life?

- need to feel secure?

Spiritual problems may require consultation with professional clergy. They have the advantage of being widely available with predictable office hours. Many are open on Sunday.

Guidelines for Choosing the Right Professional

The basic difference between the various types of mental health professionals is the extent of their training and their ability to prescribe medicine. Only psychiatrists can prescribe medication; social workers and psychologists cannot. Aside from this difference, they can all provide psychotherapy. But they may not all be the right person to give you and your family the help you need. It is often easier to choose a doctor than it is to find a mental health specialist, as medical problems usually give a clearer indication where the trouble lies. Following are some guidelines to help you choose the right counselor.

- *Make sure the professional is knowledgeable about drug addiction.* You may need to question prospective therapists about their training in drug addiction, and their feelings about and experience with 12-step recovery programs. Too often, addiction is ignored as a major contributing cause to mental health problems. Joan relates her experience:

    I remember one psychiatrist I went to didn't understand that Paul's drinking was a problem. He encouraged me to go to the bars with Paul, saying that Paul was lonely. That was fine, but where do you find a babysitter at 8:30 on a Tuesday night? Instead of going to bars and leaving my kids with sitters I didn't really know, I wish I had been going to Al-Anon earlier.

- *Ask about all medications.* Just because a doctor has an MD does not mean that person necessarily understands addiction. Says Joan,

    Paul went to a doctor for a back problem. The doctor gave him a muscle relaxant and a renewable prescription for Xanax. When I called the doctor and told him that Paul was a drug addict, he told me that none of the medicine was addictive, which was completely untrue.

- *Ask whether the mental health professional is licensed.* Be an alert consumer: ask about the qualifications of the person giving you help. She should be licensed by the state you live in to do what it is you are asking her to do. It is important that your professional has a license, not only to ensure that you will receive good service, but also to be certain that your insurance company will reimburse you for the services you receive.

- *Be certain that you like the professional's approach.* This is a concern in the mental health field, where there are a number of approaches to dealing with specific problems. Some therapists will use more reflective psychotherapy; others will use strategic approaches or behavioral modifications You may need to experience a specific approach to know if it is right for you. Remember, if you don't like the therapist's approach, you don't have to stay with him or her. Find another one with whom you are more comfortable.

What Stops Someone from Seeking Professional Help?

The authors have found that after people come to the realization that they need to seek professional help, they may postpone making an appointment. They may have come to the conclusion that they need professional help because their 12-step program is not enough, or they may not yet be in a 12-step recovery program out of fear that they cannot face a group of peers. Some may even feel that they are failures and beyond help.

Frequently, people seeking professional help are hindered by their own shame and guilt. They tend to blame themselves and to feel hopeless. Depression may even become intensified as they realize that they are not getting better. In this way, they become immobilized by their own sense of failure. This is unfortunate, for pain that could be alleviated is prolonged.

If you think that you need professional help, call a professional. They will evaluate you and give you their recommendation. The most you risk is someone validating your need for professional help. Validation of your feelings, while something that you may have little experience with, can feel great. Of course, you could also be told that you are just fine, and need only to either continue your 12-step recovery program or begin one.

Summary

Not everyone who has been affected by addiction needs professional help. But if you are concerned about the need for help, call a professional. Be good to yourself and arrange for a consultation. Either way, you win. Your feelings will be validated and you will be told you could use some professional help, or you'll be told you are just fine.

PART III

For
Professionals
and Other
Helpers

CHAPTER 13

The Lowdown on
Substance Abuse,
Child Welfare,
and the
Law

The Lowdown on Families Who Get High takes you into the world of parents/ caregivers struggling with addiction—their own, their parents/caregivers, their spouses—and gives you clear guidelines about how to speak to and work with these families, and how to address personal issues that may arise for you as you begin this process.

Legal Context

With the passage of the 1997 Adoption and Safe Families Act, or ASFA (P.L. 105–8.9), child protective workers are under incredible pressure to assess *safety* and to institute *permanency planning* within an extraordinarily short timeframe. Although permanency planning—a plan that addresses the need of the child to live in a permanent home, and not be moved from foster home to foster home—is a key concept in the child welfare field, it is a new concept to most alcohol- and drug-abuse prevention and treatment providers. Although ASFA identified the need for addiction treatment, the law provided few new resources to meet this need. Child protection workers are required to work with and find treatment for parents/ caregivers with drug abuse problems, but if this is not successful, they are mandated to terminate clients' parental rights and free their children for adoption. Therefore, substance abuse treatment providers are trying to encourage parents/caregivers choose sobriety while their clients are facing losing their children.

Being freed for adoption is a traumatic event in the life of a child, and the loss of parental rights is usually a traumatic event in the life of the parent. This phenomenon therefore must be fully understood by both fields. Now that the law requires that parental rights be terminated if reunification does not occur during a specified period of time, a major shift has occurred in our thinking about the needs of both children and their families/caregivers when substance abuse is involved. The old standard was that it is always best to try to reunite a child with his or her biological family, no matter how long it took. But ASFA reflects the realization that attempts toward reunification that stretch beyond a reasonable timeframe may be harmful to both children and their parents. Such attempts, if fruitless over a long period, harm children by prolonging their stay in foster care and may also harm parents by sending them the message that they have an unlimited time to address the issues that are interfering with their ability to nurture and care for their child.

ASFA has created a host of challenges for the child welfare, juvenile justice, and substance abuse treatment fields. The foster care system, which has always had children from addicted families, has experienced a new onslaught of children of addicts into the system as states have implemented ASFA. And the substance-abuse treatment field, which is not designed for the current influx of addicted women and their children into drug-treatment systems, is only beginning to consider how best to provide treatment to this previously underserved group. The passage of this federal law requires a common language that will create a bridge of services between these two systems.

Unfortunately, few child protective and juvenile justice workers have extensive training in substance abuse treatment, and many have none at all. Most substance-abuse professionals are unfamiliar with the child welfare and juvenile justice fields and are not aware of the new pressures being placed on parents/caregivers in care. And to further complicate matters, many of these parents/caregivers are unmotivated, destitute, or homeless, and may sincerely believe their drug use is not a problem.

What Is Addiction?

Most people believe that alcohol and drug dependence is caused by a failure of the will or by deliberate misconduct. Others believe that drug addiction is learned behavior and can be modified through specific behavioral techniques and changes in lifestyle. Still others view addiction as a symptom of an underlying emotional problem.

In reality, drug addiction is a disease as defined by the American Medical Association. Studies have proven that alcoholics are genetically predisposed to their addiction. New advances in neuroscience have discovered that the brain of an addict is permanently changed once addiction occurs.

The *Diagnostic and Statistical Manual of Mental Disorders,* by the American Psychiatric Association, (4th ed., 1994) describes substance abuse as

> *A maladaptive pattern of substance use, leading to clinically significant impairment or*
> *distress, as manifested by three (or more) of the following occurring at any time in the*
> *same 12-month period:*
> * *tolerance, as defined by either of the following:*
>   - *a need for markedly increased amounts of the substance to achieve intoxication or*
>   *desired effect*
>   - *markedly diminished effect with continued use of the same amount of the substance*
> * *withdrawal, as manifested by either of the following:*
>   - *the characteristic withdrawal syndrome for the substance*
>   - *the same (or a closely related) substance is taken to relieve or avoid withdrawal*
>   *symptoms*
> * *the substance is often taken in larger amounts or over a longer period than was intended*
> * *there is a persistent desire or unsuccessful efforts to cut down or control substance use*
> * *a great deal of time is spent in activities necessary to obtain the substance, use the*
>   *substance, or recover from its effects*
> * *important social, occupational, or recreational activities are given up or reduced be-*
>   *cause of substance use*
> * *the substance use is continued despite knowledge of having a persistent or recurrent*
>   *physical or psychological problem that is likely to have been caused or exacerbated by*
>   *the substance (e.g., current cocaine use despite recognition of cocaine induced de-*
>   *pression, or continued drinking despite the recognition that an ulcer was made worse*
>   *by alcohol consumption).*

Treatment for addicts can be a complicated process. Age, gender, drug of choice, socioeconomic status, and physical health all play a role in considering treatment options. Many types of treatment exist, including detoxification, long- and short-term inpatient treatment, methadone maintenance, and intensive and nonintensive outpatient treatment. Furthermore, the progression of treatment is frequently not smooth. Treatment for the drug abuser is a process that happens over time and may include relapse episodes as part of the recovery process.

Treatment is further complicated by mental health factors, such as Posttraumatic Stress Disorder (PTSD). PTSD can have many sources, such as sexual assault or violence. For example, many women in drug treatment have been sexually abused or assaulted at some point in their lives. And because of lifestyle issues and the impaired judgment that frequently accompanies addiction, most addicts and their children have witnessed or have been victims of domestic violence and other forms of violence, or have witnessed violence in their communities, such as drive-by shootings. These terrorizing events often create PSTD or other psychiatric problems, such as depression, which, if left untreated, may lead to relapse.

The Impact of Addiction on the Child Welfare System

Addiction has finally been recognized as a major contributing factor to the increased need for child welfare services.

- Kelleher, Chaffin, Hollenberg, and Fischer (1994) state that children whose parents or caregivers abuse drugs, including alcohol, are almost three times likelier to be abused and more than four times likelier to be neglected than those whose parents do not.

- *Blending Perspectives and Building Common Ground: A Report to Congress on Substance Abuse and Child Protection* (USDHHS, 1999), asserts that "11% of U.S. children, 8.3 million, live with at least one parent who is either alcoholic, or in need of treatment for the abuse of illicit drugs. Of these, 3.8 million live with a parent who is alcoholic, 2.1 million live with a parent whose primary problem is with illicit drugs, and 2.4 million live with a parent who abuses alcohol and illicit drugs in combination."

- It has been estimated that between 50% and 90% of all child welfare cases are alcohol- or drug-involved. Substance abuse or addiction causes or directly contributes to child maltreatment in an estimated 70% of cases, and substance abuse is estimated to be a factor in three-fourths of all placements (Young, Gardner, & Dennis, 1998).

- The U.S. General Accounting Office found that parental substance abuse was a factor for 78% of the children entering foster care in Los Angeles, New York City, and Philadelphia County (GAO, 1994).

- One survey estimated that parental chemical dependency is a contributing factor in the out-of-home placement of at least 53% of child protection cases. In another survey of families reported to CPS, in 55% of the families followed, one or both of the caretakers were identified as having a substance abuse problem, and recurrences were reported in just over half of these families (Wolock & Magura, 1996).

- According to Young, Gardner, and Dennis (1998), 40–80% of families in the child welfare system have problems with alcohol and other drugs, and those problems are connected with the abuse and neglect experienced by their children.

- More than two thirds (67%) of child maltreatment cases involve a substance-abusing parent (Jaudes et al., 1995). Wang & Daro (1997) found that for two consecutive years, more than three-fourths of states (80% in 1995 and 76% in 1996) reported that substance abuse was one of the top two conditions assessed as problems for families reported for maltreatment.

- The cost of this problem is immense, according to the National Center on Addiction and Substance Abuse at Columbia University (1999). Substance abuse and addiction account for some $10 billion in federal, state and local government spending.

The Four Timetables

Four timetables impact drug-affected families and, as a result, affect professionals working with addicted families.

1. In most states, the child welfare system requires a permanency hearing after 12 months; some states have a timetable of six months. This means that in most cases, caseworkers are trying to do permanency planning, parenting education, and arrange for drug treatment simultaneously.

2. The Temporary Assistance for Needy Families (TANF) programs mandates clients to find work in 24 months. This means that the federal dollars available to help troubled families are time limited.

3. Treatment and recovery have their own timetables. Recovery is a process that happens over time, and it sometimes takes years. Drug treatment is not a process that fits neatly into a predictable, organized timeframe. Many times, relapse is part of the process of recovery.

4. Finally, children, especially young children, have a developmental timetable. The current research on brain development shows that the first 18 months of an infant's life are critical to his or her future development. This is also the key time for bonding and attachment to caregivers. This means that the longer we postpone permanency planning, the more likely it is that children's healthy development will be compromised, thus potentially creating future difficulties for children who are already severely challenged.

Special Challenges for Child Welfare and Substance Abuse Professionals

Given these concerns, it would seem that the only way to effectively deal with the impact that substance abuse has on the child welfare, juvenile justice, and foster care systems is for child protection, child care, and drug-treatment professionals to join together to work with these troubled families. Yet child welfare and substance abuse professionals rarely work together and in fact are often hostile to each other's point of view. The authors have found that this is usually due to the fact that so many professionals in both the child welfare and substance abuse fields have personal experiences with addiction, physical and emotional abuse and neglect, and/or domestic violence. These may be childhood experiences with a parent or caregiver, or they may be factors in current or past adult relationships, or in past relationships.

For such individuals, dealing with these issues at the professional level may give rise to painful memories, or may underscore current personal dilemmas that they are facing. While not the primary intention of the authors, it is hoped that this book may also serve to assist these professionals in their own personal journeys through these issues.

It is the authors' hope that this book will be a bridge for all the disciplines involved with addicted families—a bridge to family reunification, substance abuse recovery, and a catalyst for the development of healthy families for clients and those working with them.

CHAPTER 14

Engaging Families and Caregivers Affected by Substance Abuse

Frequently, when children enter the child welfare or juvenile justice systems, the adults charged with their care do not immediately understand the context of these children's lives. The reality is that children who enter either system due to substance abuse in their families may have been physically and sexually abused or severely emotionally maltreated, or they may have been one of the financial supports of an otherwise destitute family; they may have been abandoned and watched helplessly as the family of their childhood has fallen apart around them, or they may have watched a friend or family member be killed in a drive-by shooting or other violent act. The children and adolescents who are referred to treatment, or whose parents are referred, often come to us having been denied the gift of an innocent childhood. They come to us having felt unsafe in their homes, their schools, and their communities—and this they show in their actions.

In other words, these children and adolescents come to us not just due to substance abuse problems—their own or those of a parent—but due to the fact that they have been traumatized. As a result of this trauma, they are demonstrating to us and to society that they cannot cope, that they need and demand help.

Unfortunately, substance abuse is just one of the problems faced by a majority of the families who are referred for services. Many of the children, adolescents, and adults served by the substance abuse, child welfare, juvenile justice, and mental health systems present with a vast array of emotional as well as behavioral difficulties. Behavioral problems are often the precipitating factor in the referral, especially with adolescents. They are characterized as angry, poor school performers, resistant, even defiant. Not until they are in the child welfare or juvenile justice system is the substance abuse of their parents or caregivers identified. Given the vast array of problems that children and adolescents present with, however, it can actually be a benefit when substance abuse problems are in the mix, for we do know how to deal with these issues.

Substance Abuse Screening

To determine whether a family member or caregiver has a substance abuse problem, the family member should be screened. Substance abuse screening is helpful in determining whether a full substance abuse assessment is warranted. If so, this fuller assessment can be conducted by a substance abuse professional. You can conduct a screening by using the following questions, commonly referred to as the CAGE questions.

During the last 12 months, have you ever:

- felt you ought to Cut down on your drinking or drug use?

- been Annoyed when people criticized your drinking or drug use?

- felt bad or Guilty about your drinking or drug use?

- felt the need for an Eye-opener—that is, awakened wanting a drink or another drug?

If you get a 'yes' response to one or more questions, consider referring the client and his or her family for a full assessment.

Understanding Substance Abuse: All in the Family

If your screening determines that substance abuse is an issue in a client's family, then it is important to begin to understand just what makes these families tick.

Substance abuse is a very common factor that brings children and families into the child welfare system. The person with the addiction may be a family member or the adolescent. No matter who the person with a substance abuse problem is, the support that they receive from their family is one vital factor that will assist them in achieving recovery.

This means that substance abuse is best approached from a *family-systems* viewpoint. What does this mean? This means that all family members will require interventions, not just the active substance user. Treatment plans and goals are written not just for the child or adolescent who may be using, but also for the family member who may be using, to encourage their attendance in treatment. Goals may need to specify that a family member go to a 12-step recovery program such as Alcoholics Anonymous (AA), or Narcotics Anonymous (NA). In addition, one goal must be that family members attend meetings of a 12-step program such as Al-Anon, where the focus is living with or caring about someone with addiction—even if these family members are already involved in a treatment program for their own addiction, or even if they need their own addiction treatment but are resistant. Likewise, children are encouraged to attend Alateen, a self-help program for adolescents affected by addiction, even if they are involved in their own substance abuse treatment.

Why this insistence on treatment for all family members and caregivers? Because substance abuse affects all the members of a family in many predictable ways.

Family Rules

While there is a genetic basis to the disease of addiction, the ways that families adapt to living with this disease are learned. And one important treatment intervention is to change how families and caregivers deal with this disease.

To begin to understand this, we must first look at how families operate. All families seek to continue as a unit. Members seek to preserve their relationships with one another and their group identity. They have expected standards of behavior. These expectations usually take the form of family rules, which serve to let the family members know how to behave and what to think, even what to believe. These rules even spell out how problems will be solved and what solutions are acceptable or unacceptable.

Similarly, addicted families have rules, unwittingly taught from one generation to the next, and unconsciously obeyed. Unfortunately for the tens of millions affected by alcoholism and drug addiction, in the addicted family, these rules are often not perceived as problematic or as having painful consequences. They are the norm for *this* family, and as loyal members of this family, each member will follow them. These rules keep family members connected, protect the family unit, and help to form the family's unique identity, both as a unit and as individuals. The child learns the family's rules, and by learning and practicing what their family holds to be true, they remain attached, connected, part of the family.

These rules often remain largely unconscious, and are frequently undiscussed. One reason for this is the human reality that once an individual has the conscious knowledge of painful consequences, he or she feels compelled to change, and change can be frightening. In this instance, change could serve to distance—or even to remove—the individual from his or her family (O'Gorman, 1994).

Two Sets of Rules to Cover Any Contingency

If one is good, two must be better, or so it seems with the typical alcoholic family. The alcoholic family operates with two sets of rules, one for each of the two cycles found in the family. Each cycle has its own set of rules that cover the behaviors typically found in this cycle.

The first cycle is the wet cycle when the parent/caregiver is drinking. The second is the dry cycle, when the alcoholic parent or spouse is not drinking (Bowen, 1974).

To understand how alcoholism affects the family you are working with, you need to distinguish the differences in the way *this* family functions when the alcoholic is drinking, and also when he or she is not. Another way of saying this is that for each question you ask a family, there may be two answers, depending on which part of the cycle they are answering from.

In the typical alcoholic family, when the alcoholic is drinking (or the drug addict is using), the family is more engaged. Not only may family members play music, for example, but they may play it in loud tones, and the TV may be blasting as well. Family discussions, which may have been few on the dry side, now begin. There are more interactions, more physical contact, and more eye contact. But as the drinking continues, this contact often takes a negative turn. Speaking may become yelling, and physical contact may move from hugging to hurting.

Nevertheless, it is on this side of the cycle that the family interacts with one another. There is contact here, and for this reason this part of the cycle is called the *intimacy ritual*. It is during this part of the cycle that the family members learn this family's rules for making contact and being close. The intimacy ritual develops despite its obvious negativity, for there are many secondary gains attached to what, on the surface, look like only negative behaviors. Studies have shown that it is more painful to live alienated from those around you than even to be connected in a painful manner (Bowen, 1974). So being close at any cost is the driving force that perpetuates the cycle of abuse in the alcoholic family. As difficult or downright bloody the contact may be, the family maintains the rules that allow it, for having no contact is even more painful, as you will see in the dry cycle.

The dry cycle has been likened to walking on eggshells without breaking any, and similarly, as the feeling you have when you are running out of air but are afraid to gasp. The dry cycle is noted by the absence of contact. It is characterized by withdrawal, for family members fear that any contact, any gesture, will precipitate another drinking/drugging episode. The guilt and fear associated with this is enough to drive family members away from one another. They may stop talking and will spend less time together. No one wants to be responsible for triggering the alcoholic into drinking, as the alcoholic's drinking is always blamed on someone who is doing something wrong. Consequently, family members are also driven away from their own feelings, as they withdraw and repress them in order to protect themselves and their family's temporary peace.

In essence, family members who live with addiction have learned two sets of rules: Rules for the wet cycle, when contact is permitted and nurtured, but more often than not is negative and painful; and rules for the dry cycle, when contact is not allowed, and is even punished by guilt and total responsibility for the substance use that ensues.

Learned Helplessness

One of the most unfortunate consequences for children of parents/caregivers with addictions, is the tendency of children reared in these families to learn to be helpless. This is due to the family's conflicting sets of rules, the child's need to learn to depend on outside cues in order to determine how to act and which set of rules needs to be followed, and how the family extracts loyalty to its rules.

These rules and the accompanying family dynamics inevitably teach the child to be helpless, which is in contrast to how children naturally function. The infant's first need is to master its environment. A child's first success in mastery is to cry to relieve hunger pains. Children learn that by crying, they can relieve their distress. By learning how to relieve that distress, they begin to influence and eventually master their environment. The need for mastery over the environment is a life task. At different points in a child's development, mastery over his environment is demonstrated in a variety of ways. For example, the striving for good school grades and the development of a fierce competitive spirit, as seen at high school and college sports' events, to perhaps, the thrill of stealing and not getting caught. Mastery is a natural part of development. In the alcoholic family, however, the family's rules interfere with this natural tendency to want to master, and often can produce a different result that we call *learned helplessness*.

Children learn helplessness as a result of living in a family where a behavior is rewarded at some times and punished at others (Seligman, 1990). In families with addiction, learning the right behavior is a complex task because it is constantly changing. The center of the child's world in such families is frequently the addict, and the perceptive child learns how to watch the family as a whole so that whatever the circumstances—whether the alcoholic parent is drunk, hungover, or dry—the child will know how to act. When the cues keep shifting and the consequences for mistakes are severe, the child becomes traumatized and as a result, may become dependent on these external cues in order to know what to do (O'Gorman, 1975). The child's emotional energy and time is therefore focused on others rather than on learning to understand what her own needs are and how to address them. Consequently, children in these families often learn not to follow their feelings or their own sense of right and wrong, but rather, to follow the actions of others—to *react*, based on how a particular situation is being defined, as opposed to learning to *act* based upon their own judgment (Conger, et al., 1992). Eventually children learn not to trust themselves and their own perceptions at all, but rather to trust the viewpoints of others, and even to the point of denying their own reality (Oliver-Diaz & O'Gorman, 1988).

The brighter the child, the more in tune with his environment he is, the more anxious he will likely become. Children will frequently be punished and become confused until they learn the addicted family rule of not depending on themselves, but rather reading the cues around them and agreeing with their parent's interpretation of reality. This need to trust the reality of another can be illustrated by the following common scenarios:

- an intoxicated parent asserting that she has not been drinking;

- a mother with a black eye stating that *no,* her husband did not hit her;

- a parent blacking out—that is, having amnesia—and not remembering promises that he made to his child while he was using, or that he beat his child, and insisting that the child made it all up.

Over time, children also learn to generalize this helplessness beyond just dependency on others, to a dependency on something outside of themselves. This belief that feeling good or comfortable can only come from a source outside of one's self, causes many children of substance abusers to rely on others and not on themselves in relationships. And these same children, who have a genetic predisposition to develop addiction, may begin to experiment with drinking, or using drugs, in part because they are anxious and want to see if this will create a problem for them. Of course, their initial use will probably not resemble full-blown addiction, and so many high-risk children relax into a use pattern that quickly becomes problematic. Not only is substance use part of the family's schema of problem solving, but it is also a family-sanctioned way of giving oneself pleasure, a way of escape, and a way of fulfilling the need for attention, as the user is frequently the center of attention in the family. Drinking or drugging is one way to make sure that you are seen, and that you belong.

Learned helplessness can also lead to other types of behaviors. These behaviors include the tendencies to:

- develop cripplingly dependent relationships;

- compulsively overeat, work, shop, and/or gamble; and

- compulsively pursue sex, but find in it only relief from tension, not joy.

To begin to understand just how the family you are working with is organizing around addiction, fill out the diagram (Figure 1) on the following page with them.

How to Engage Families Affected by Addiction in Helpful Conversations

"From small beginnings come great things."

—Dutch proverb

Speaking to parents/caregivers about addiction will be easier if you understand what motivates them. Change is a process, not an event, and this process is composed of

FIGURE 1. Wet/Dry Model

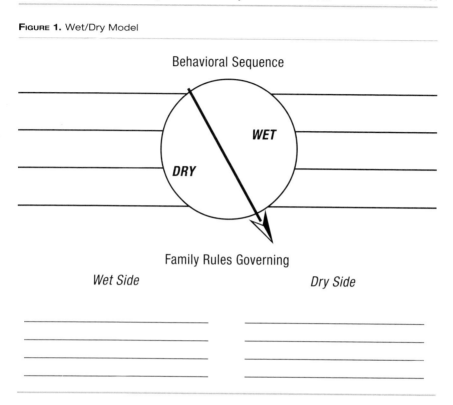

Behavioral Sequence

WET

DRY

Family Rules Governing

Wet Side   *Dry Side*

several steps, all of which begin with how you approach a family/caregiver in need. How you begin to speak to a family in trouble will often determine how well that family will understand what you have to say and how motivated they will be by your assessment and recommendations. From such small beginnings are built the foundations of a therapeutic relationship.

Helpful conversations begin with a genuine interest in knowing what is positive and working well in your clients' lives. But it is important to understand that being curious about what is working well in someone's life is not meant to minimize their pain or confusion. In fact, you need to begin your conversations by understanding what the problem is, from your client's perspective.

Understanding the Problem from the Client's Viewpoint

Understanding the problem—the removal of children, arrest, conviction, termination of parental rights, and/or mandate to go to treatment—from the parent/caregiver's point of view is a critical first step of a treatment intervention. The following questions can help you begin to understand your client's point of view. Put these thoughts into your own words, or use these questions as written, and vary them to suit your own communication style:

- What brought you here?

- What happened?

- How do you see this problem?

- Is it a good thing that you are here?

- How do you feel about this problem?

Approaching a problem from your client's viewpoint allows them to feel understood. It decreases their resistance and increases the possibility that you will be able to be effective in reaching them. This is important, since one problem that caring professionals face is that by the time that a family enters the child welfare, mental health, or substance abuse system, they have become defensive about what others see as *wrong* with them. This is because these systems have had a tendency to become focused on the problems—what is wrong with the family—and often do not spend the same amount of time focusing on the solutions, or what is right. It is important to remember that when we focus on problems, we tend to elicit more resistance.

Helpful conversations begin by working with clients on their *internal dialogue*, or what they think and feel about themselves, and culminate when you have developed a genuine interest in knowing what is positive and working well in their lives. To move from a problem-focused orientation to a solution-focused one, you will need to go beyond traditional assessment techniques and determine what motivates a client. When we focus on solutions, we become curious about the following:

- If the problem went away, what would be different?

- What is the first thing that would indicate to you that the problem no longer existed?

- How would you feel in this scenario?

How Families/Caregivers Want to Be Seen: The Preferred View

A key component of being able to reach your clients is the ability to understand their strengths. This engagement technique, based upon the work of Eron and Lund (1996), deals with understanding how clients are connected to other people in two scenarios: when they are at their best—that is, when others perceive the family members as they wish to be seen (their *preferred view*); and when they are not at their best—when the way that others perceive them makes the family members uncomfortable in some way (their *nonpreferred view*).

First, you'll need to find out how families want to be viewed by others—their preferred view of themselves. From here, you can seek to motivate changes in their behavior by inquiring about the feelings and consequences of being seen in ways that make them feel appreciated, safe, and secure, versus ways that do not make them feel good or safe. This can be helpful for families affected by addiction, who may have a long history of deluding others and trying to delude themselves into believing that there is no problem. This approach also allows you to engage and understand families based on how the family understands itself, thus allowing room for cultural sensitivity, among other advantages

The following list of questions will provide a starting point for you to begin to get to know the families you are working with in a new and more positive manner. These questions are simply a guide; you don't need to ask all of them, and you don't need to ask all of them at once. Helpful conversations can take place over a series of interviews.

As you begin along this line of inquiry, you will probably think of few questions that that you want to ask that are not on this list. Go ahead and use them. Remember, this is an engagement technique that will allow you to gain the information you need help the children and families you work with move toward positive outcomes.

- How happy are you now with your life? Your family life?

- When have you been happy with your life and your family life?

- What is working well?

- What has worked well in the past?

- How well are you accomplishing what you would like as a family or an individual?

- What would you like to accomplish in the next year?

- What is one thing that would you closer to your goal?

- Who could help you move closer to your goal?

- What could that person do to be helpful?

- What goals have you accomplished in the past?

- Who has helped you accomplish these goals?

- What have they done that has been helpful?

- What skills have been helpful in accomplishing these goals?

- How do you want to be treated?

- Who treats you this way, or has treated you this way? How does it feel?

- What feels different when you are treated in this way?

- What is one of the ways in which you are strong? In which your family is strong?

- Do you (or does your family) use this now?

- When you do this, who notices?

- How does it feel?

- Did you use it in the past? When? How did it feel?

- What is one of your skills? One of your family's skills?

- When are you likely to use this skill? When is your family likely to use it?

- Who notices when you use this skill?

- How long have you had this skill?

- How does it feel it use it?

- What do you like to do, and why?

- Who do you like to do with it?

- How does this activity make you feel?

- How would you describe yourself? Your family?

- What is your best quality?

From these types of questions, move towards discovering which parts of their life reinforce their view of themselves.

- What do others say is the best quality you have? Your family has?

- How does it make you feel to be seen in this way?

- Tell me about your friends. What do they do?

- What do your friends say about you?

- What do your friends think is working well in your life?

- What do your friends think is your best quality? Your best accomplishment?

- Are there people in your life who see you or your family in ways that make you feel good?

- Who are they, and what do they see?

- How does it feel to be seen in this way?

- Are their people who see you or your family using some of your strengths? Who are they?

- How does it feel to be seen in ways that make you feel good?

- Are there people in your life who inspire you to accomplish what you would like to do? Who are they?

- What do they inspire you to accomplish?

- Are there people in your life that inspire you to use your strengths? Who are they?

- What strengths do they inspire you to use?

- Are there qualities these people see in you that you like? What are they?

- Are there things you do that these people see and appreciate? What are they?

- What effect does it have on you to be noticed and appreciated?

- Are there people in your life who inspire you to accomplish what you would like to do? Who are they?

- Are there qualities these people see in you that you like?

- Are there things you do that these people see and appreciate?

- What effect does it have on you to be noticed and appreciated?

- What effect does it have on you to be seen as using one of your strengths?

Motivating Change: The Nonpreferred View and the Gap

For families affected by substance abuse, the key to change lies in the gap between the individual or family's preferred and nonpreferred view of themselves—that is, the difference between how they *want* to be perceived by others and how they do *not* want to be perceived. It is when an individual or a family is in the gap that they are the most uncomfortable and they most desire to do something different. Ask them:

- Are there things people say about you that you do not like?

- What do they say?

- When do they say it?

- What do you not like about what they say?

- Are there people who see you in ways that you don't like?

- Who are they?

- What do they see?

- What do they say about you?

- How would you describe how these people see you?

- When you are perceived in this way, what happens?

- How does it make you feel to be seen in this way?

- What do you wish people would see or say instead?

- What do you do when you are seen in this way?

- What do you want to do?

- How does it feel when you are doing this?

The next step is to understand how to work with a family to set a goal. For a family impacted by addiction, what *they* view is the next step in terms of creating change may not be the change step that *you* see for them. Remember, change is a process composed of many steps. Each step in this process—no matter how small—should be understood, recorded, and celebrated, because every step closer to the goal makes the eventual attainment of the goal more certain, and less frightening.

Sometimes a family will see a change of actions as a possibility. Ask them:

- Are there things you are doing now that you would like to change?

- What do your friends think you should do?

- When do they think you should take this action?

Other times change may begin with a shifting of thoughts or feelings.

- Are there thoughts and feelings you would like to change?

- If you changed these things, who would you like to notice this change?

- What effect would this person's noticing your change have on you?

And so on.

This type of inquiry allows the person speaking with the family to understand not just how the family would like to be seen and treated, but also how they do *not* like to be seen, and how they do *not* like to be treated—important components to understand in determining a treatment and motivation approach. It also allows you to understand change from the family's perspective, so that you may work with them in shaping and encouraging change, and not adding to their resistance by demanding more than they can conceive of doing.

The following exercise will assist you visualizing how to approach your clients most effectively. For example, with a client who currently receives Temporary Aid to Needy Families (TANF) funds, and who also values their independence, there is obviously a gap between how they want to be viewed by others and how they feel they are viewed, at least by you. You can use this by speaking to them about their value of independence and assist them in determining how to become truly independent. You could use this information to create treatment interventions that allow you to speak to them about how surprised you are that someone who so values independence allows themselves to be dependent on drugs. You can help them reduce the gap between how they want to be treated and how they feel others treat them.

To help make this even clearer, list the client's responses in the following way (see Figure 2). Make three columns. Keep listing attributes of the family until you think you have grasped their particular unique preferred view, their nonpreferred view, and the gap between the two.

The key in this approach is to:

· begin where your clients are

· become curious about what they see as their strengths and their challenges

· speak to them with respect

· speak to them about their strengths, their dreams, their vision for the future

· point out the inconsistency between how they wish to be seen and the situations they keep putting themselves in that cause others to view them in a less favorable light.

Resilience: Teaching Clients to Bounce Back

In order to speak to our clients about their preferred view of themselves, it is important to have a language concerning their strengths, their resiliency. Resilience is the ability to bounce back from the adversities that life throws at each of us. It is knowing that one can survive, and even take pride in that survival.

Many of the clients we serve have suffered unspeakable horrors. Some have seen a parent murdered, or have a parent in prison. Many have grown up in families where their parent's addiction meant that they did not receive the proper care. Others have been sexually abused by an adult for whom they cared deeply, and who they thought cared for them.

But seeing clients as resilient is not to deny the pain of the abuse, neglect, traumas, and maltreatment many of them have endured. Although clients may have

FIGURE 2. Motivating Change

Preferred View	Gap	Nonpreferred View
Who sees them in this way?		*Who sees them in this way?*
How does it feel to be seen in this way?		*How does it feel to be seen in this way?*
What are they doing when they are seen in a way that makes them feel good?		*What are they doing when they are seen in a way that does not make them feel good?*

been victimized, seeing them as resilient means that we do not perceive them as victims. Rather, we see them as survivors that can be nurtured into developing pride in their own ability to survive.

Coupled with this concept of resilience is the understanding that your clients are not damaged, but have sustained challenges. In the traditional mental health Damage Model, clients are viewed as having succumbed to the negative influences around them. In the Challenge Model, however, a client can be depicted as having *rebounded* from the negative influences in their lives (Wolin & Wolin, 1993). This is an empowering concept that gives hope to the child, the family, and the helper, and helps develop pride in the child and family's achievements. The development of this survivor's pride is at the center of many efforts in the treatment of substance abuse.

So often our training is to focus on only what is wrong, but to bring about change, particularly change with high-risk families, we need to also focus on what is right. The work of Drs. Steve and Sybil Wolin can greatly assist us in doing this. In their book, *The Resilient Self* (1993), they describe seven core resiliencies. They are:

- *Insight:* The skill of asking tough questions and giving honest answers.

- *Independence:* The ability to draw boundaries between yourself and a troubled parent; learning to keep safe emotional and physical distance.

- *Relationships:* The gift of developing intimate and fulfilling ties to other people that balance a regard for your needs and empathy for another.

- *Initiative:* The ability to take charge of problems and exert control; a taste for stretching and testing yourself in demanding tasks.

- *Creativity:* The ability to impose order, beauty, and purpose on the chaos of troubling experiences and painful feelings.

- *Humor:* The ability to find the comic in the tragic.

- *Morality:* The development of an informed conscience that translates into a desire for a good personal life to others.

As you assess your clients' problems, also assess their strengths, and remember that resilience is not a static quality. As O'Gorman (1994) notes in her book *Dancing Backwards in High Heels: How Women Master the Art of Resilience,* one person may use different styles of resiliency at various times depending on his or her circumstances, and on what he or she is bouncing back from. The following are the most commonly used styles of resilience:

- *Stellar:* individual is challenged, but knows that she can survive

- *Paradoxical:* resilient, but only using these skills in one aspect of his life

- *Overwhelmed:* individual is unable to access resiliency due to trauma

- *Underdeveloped:* individual's resiliency skills are not fully developed

- *Self-contained:* individual's identity is tied into being resilient to the exclusion of other aspects of herself

- *Balanced:* individual is able to access resiliency when he needs it

Become familiar with the different styles of resilience, as many of the families who come to us are strong, but they may be overwhelmed by the circumstances that they are currently facing, including addiction, poverty, and violence. In terms of strengths, this means that they are that they are constantly moving, trying to adjust, trying to make their lives work in more productive ways. It is important to understand this concept of movement when we speak about strengths, for it is this movement between different styles of coping that allows clients—and indeed, all of us—to develop responses that allow us to utilize our strengths no matter what is before us.

Glossary

- *Drug addiction*—A disease, generally genetically transmitted, in which one becomes physically and psychologically addicted to alcohol and/or prescribed or illegal drugs, such as Valium, Librium, cocaine, marijuana, or heroin.

- *Compulsive gambling*—An addiction, much like drug addiction, in which the individual cannot control his or her compulsive need to bet.

- *Eating disorders*—Compulsive and addictive behaviors that range from compulsive overeating to self-starvation (anorexia), to bingeing and purging (bulimia).

- *Familial drug addiction*—A pattern of family functioning in which family members are organized around and adapted to the addictive and/or compulsive behavior of one or more members of their family system. It is a pattern of family functioning which is predictable and painful, adheres to rigid rules of behavior that constrict the expression of feelings, and is often replicated in subsequent generations.

- *Recovery*—The process of reorganizing one's life so that it is no longer centered on an addiction or compulsion, including alcohol and other drug use, gambling, and other compulsions. For the adult child of the addicted or compulsive family or the spouse of an addict, recovery means no longer being centered on the addict or how the addiction has affected them.

- *Learned helplessness*—A type of behavior, unconsciously taught to children from birth, in which children's needs are consistently fulfilled by something or someone beyond themselves. This leads to a lack of independent action, as the individual's energy becomes focused on the person or the activity on which the dependency is centered, rather than on taking care of him or herself. Learned helplessness increases the likelihood that someone with a genetic predisposition to develop drug addiction will begin to abuse substances, and also leads to other types of compulsive dependent behaviors such as those noted in adult children of drug addicts. These behaviors include the tendency to:

  — develop cripplingly dependent relationships,

  — compulsively overeat, work, shop, and/or gamble, and

  — compulsively pursue sex, but find on it only relief from tension, not joy.

References, Bibliography, and Suggested Reading

References

Al-Anon Family Groups. (1979). *How can I help my children?* New York: Author.

Al-Anon Family Groups. (1980). *Alateen: Hope for children of alcoholics.* New York: Author.

Al-Anon Family Groups. (1984). *An Al-Anon/Alateen member survey* (No. 292-1-84). New York: Al-Anon Family Groups.

Al-Anon Family Groups. (2001). *Alcoholics Anonymous.* New York: Author.

Al-Anon Family Groups. (2004). *Twelve steps and twelve traditions.* New York: Author.

American Psychiatric Association. (1980). *Diagnostic and statistical manual of mental disorders* (3rd ed.). Washington, DC: Author.

American Psychiatric Association. (1994). *Diagnostic and statistical manual of mental disorders* (4th ed.). Washington, DC: Author.

Anthony, E. J. (1974). The syndrome of the psychologically invulnerable child. In E. J. Anthony & C. Koupernick (Eds.), *The child in his family* (Vol. 3, pp. 529–544). New York: John Wiley.

Bell, R. (1998). *Changing bodies, changing lives: A book for teens on sex and relationships* (Third Edition). New York: Random House.

Bepko, C., & Krestan, J. (1985). *The responsibility trap.* New York: Free Press.

Black, C. (1979). Children of drug addicts. *Alcohol Health and Research World, 4*(1), 23–27.

Black, C. (1981). *It will never happen to me.* Denver, CO: Medical Administration.

Black, C. (1985). *Repeat after me: Workbook for adult children.* Denver, CO: Medical Administration.

Bowen, M. (1974). Alcoholism as viewed through family systems theory and family psychotherapy. *Annals New York Academy of Science, 233*, 115–122.

Brohl, K. (1996). *Working with traumatized children: A handbook for healing.* Washington, DC: Child Welfare League of America.

Brohl, K., & Case-Potter, J., (2004). *When your child has been molested: A parents' guide to healing and recovery.* San Francisco: Jossey-Bass.

Campbell, S. (1984). *Beyond the power struggle.* San Luis Obispo, CA: Impact.

Cermak, T. A. (1985). *Primer on adult children of drug addicts.* Deerfield Beach, FL: Health Communications, Inc.

Chess, S., Thomas, A., & Birch, H. (1976). *Your child is a person: A psychological approach to parenting without guilt.* New York: Penguin Books.

Conger, R. D., Conger, K. J., Elder, G. H., Lorenz, F. O., Simons, R. I., & Whitbeck, L. B. (1992). A family process of economic hardship and adjustment of early adolescent boys. *Child Development, 63*, 526–541.

Dies, R. R., & Burghardt, K. (1991). Group interventions for children of alcoholics: Prevention and treatment in the schools. *Journal of Adolescent Group Therapy, 1*, 219–234.

Earls, F., Reich, W., Jung, K. G., & Cloninger, C. R. (1998). Psychopathology in children of alcoholic and antisocial parents. *Alcoholism: Clinical and Experimental Research, 12*, 481–487.

el Guebaly, N., & Offord, D. R. (1997). The offspring of alcoholics: A critical review. *American Journal of Psychiatry, 134*, 357–365.

Erikson, E. H. (1963). *Childhood and society.* New York: Norton.

Eron, J. B., & Lund, T. W. (1996). *Narrative solutions in brief therapy.* New York: Guilford.

Evans, K., & Sullivan, J. (1995). *Treating addicted survivors of trauma.* New York: Guilford.

Famularo, R., Kinscherff, R., & Fenton, T. (1992). Parental substance abuse and the nature of child maltreatment. *Child Abuse & Neglect, 16*.

Finn, P., & O'Gorman, P. (1981). *Teaching about alcohol.* Boston: Allyn and Bacon.

Gardner, R. (1976). *Psychotherapy with children of divorce.* New York: Aronson.

Gravitz, H. L., & Bowden, J. D. (1985). *Guide to recovery: A book for adult children of drug addicts.* Holmes Beach, FL: Learning.

Hill, J. P., & Lynch, M. E. (1983). The intensification of gender-related role expectations during early adolescence. In J. Brooks-Gunn & A. C. Petersen (Eds.), *Girls at puberty* (pp. 201–228). New York: Plenum Press.

James, J. E., & Goldman, M. (1971). Behavior trends of wives of drug addicts. *Quarterly Journal of Studies on Alcohol, 32*, 373–381.

Jaudes, P., Ekwo, E., & Van Voohis, J. (1995, September). Association of drug abuse and child abuse. *Child Abuse and Neglect, 19*(9), 1065–1075.

Kelleher, K., Chaffin, M., Hollenberg, M., & Fischer, E. (1994). Alcohol and drug disorders among physically abusive and neglectful parents in a community-based sample. *American Journal of Public Health, 84*, 1586–1590.

Kumpfer, K. L. (1999). Outcome measures of interventions in the study of children of substance-abusing parents. *Pediatrics, 103*, 1128–1144.

Kumpfer, K. L., & DeMarsh, J. (1986). Family environmental and genetic influences on children's future chemical dependency. In S. Ezekoye, K. L. Kumpfer, & W. Bukoski (Eds.), *Childhood and chemical abuse, prevention and intervention*. New York: Haworth Press.

Lewis, C., & Lewis, M. A. (1984). Peer pressure and risk-taking behaviors in children. *American Journal of Public Health, 74*, 580–584.

McCall, R. B. (1979). *Infants*. Cambridge, MA: Harvard University Press.

Moos, R. H., & Billings, A. G. (1982). Children of alcoholics during the recovery process: Alcoholic and matched control families. *Addictive Behaviors, 7*, 155–163.

Moos, R., & Moos, B. (1984, March). The process of recovery from drug addiction: Comparing functioning in families of drug addicts and matched control families. *Journal of Studies on Alcohol, 45*.

Mussen, P. H., Conger, J. J., & Kagan, J. (1969). *Child development and personality* (3rd ed.). New York: Harper and Row.

Natasi, B. K., & DeZolt, D. M. (1994). *School interventions for children of alcoholics*. New York: Guilford.

National Center on Addiction and Substance Abuse (1999). *No safe haven: Children of substance-abusing parents*. New York: Columbia University. Available at http://www.casacolumbia.org or by calling 212/841-5227.

Nici, J. (1979). Wives of drug addicts as repeaters. *Journal of Studies on Alcohol, 40*, 677-682.

O'Gorman, P. (1975). *Self-concept, locus of control, perception of father in adolescents in severe problem drinking, recovering drug addict, and non–drug addict homes*. Unpublished doctoral dissertation, Fordham University, New York.

O'Gorman, P. (1984). Alateen—Why refer? A psychologists' viewpoint. In *Al-Anon faces drug addiction* (2nd ed., pp. 55–62). New York: Al-Anon Family Group Headquarters.

O'Gorman, P. (1994). *Dancing backwards in high heels: How women master the art of resilience*. Center City, MN: Hazelden.

O'Gorman, P. (2004, January/February) The anatomy of resilience: what makes some clients bounce back better than others?. *Counselor: The Magazine for Addiction Professionals 5* (1), pp. 14-17.

O'Gorman, P., & Lacks, H. (1979). *Aspects of youthful drinking*. New York: National Council on Drug Addiction.

O'Gorman, P., & Oliver-Diaz, P. (1987) *Breaking the cycle of addiction*. Deerfield Beach, FL: Health Communications, Inc.

O'Gorman, P., & Ross, R. (1986). Children of drug addicts in the juvenile justice system, In R. Ackerman (Ed.), *Growing in the shadow: Children of drug addicts*. Deerfield Beach, FL: Health Communications, Inc.

Oliver-Diaz, P. (1984). Self-help groups through children's eyes. *Focus on Family and Chemical Dependency, 8*(2), 28–29, 38.

Oliver-Diaz, P., & O'Gorman, P. (1988). *12 steps to self-parenting*. Deerfield Beach, FL: Health Communications, Inc.

Papp, P. (1983). *The process of change*. New York: Guilford.

Reid, J., Macchetto, P., & Foster, S. (1999). *No safe haven: Children of substance-abusing parents*. New York: Columbia University Center on Addiction and Substance Abuse.

Rice, E., Ekdahl, M., & Miller, L. (1971). *Children of mentally ill parents*. New York: Behavioral.

Rosen, H. (1980). *The development of sociomoral knowledge: A cognitive structural approach*. New York: Columbia University Press.

Russel M., Strasburger, E. L., Welte, J. W., & Blume, S. B. (1983). Factors associated with coping in successful adult children of drug addicts. *Drug Addiction: Clinical and Experimental Research, 7*(120).

Schaefer, C. (1982). *How to influence children: A complete guide for becoming a better parent*. New York: Van Nostrand Reinhold.

Schaeffer, H. R. (1971). *The growth of sociability*. Harmondsworth, UK: Penguin Press.

Schor, E. M. D. (Ed.). (1999). *Caring for your school age-child*. New York: American Academy of Pediatrics.

Seligman, M. (1990). *Learned optimism*. New York: Pocket Books.

Selvini-Palazzoli, M. (1978). *Self-starvation: From individuation to family therapy in the treatment of anorexia nervosa*. New York: Aronson.

Shelov, S. (1998). *Caring for your baby and young child: Birth to age 5*. New York: Bantam.

Sher, K. J. (1997). Psychological characteristics of children of alcoholics. *Alcohol Health and Research World, 21*(3).

Silber, A. (1974). Rationale for the technique of psychotherapy with drug addicts, *International Journal of Psychoanalytic Psychotherapy, 3,* 28–47.

Simmons, R. G., & Rosenberg, F. (1975). Sex, sex roles, and self-image. *Journal of Youth and Adolescence, 4,* 229–258.

Spitz, R. A., & Wolf, K. M. (1946). Anaclitic depression: An inquiry into the genesis of psychiatric conditions in early childhood II. In A. Freud et al. (Eds.), *Psychoanalytic study of the child* (Vol. 2, pp. 313–342). New York: International Universities Press.

Steele, C. E. (1980). Weight loss among teenage girls: An adolescent crisis. *Adolescence, 15,* 823–829.

Steinglass, P., Bennett, L., Wolin, S., & Reiss, D. (1993). *The alcoholic family*. New York: Basic Books.

Steinglass, P., & Robertson, A. (1983). The drug addict family. In B. Kissin & H. Begleiter (Eds.), *The biology of drug addiction, Vol. 6: The pathogenesis of drug addiction: Psychosocial factors* (pp. 243–307). New York: Plenum Press.

Strauss, R. (1976). Conceptualizing drug addiction and alcohol problems. In P. O'Gorman, I. Smith, & S. Stringfield (Eds.), *Defining adolescent alcohol use: Implications toward a definition of adolescent drug addiction* (pp. 106–107). New York: National Council on Drug Addiction.

Striegel-Moore, L., Silberstein, L., & Rodin, J. (1986). Toward an understanding of risk factors for bulimia. *American Psychologist, 41,* 246–263.

U.S. Department of Health and Human Services. (1999). *Blending Perspectives and Building Common Ground: A Report to Congress on Substance Abuse and Child Protection.* Washington, DC: Government Printing Office. Available online at http://aspe.hhs.gov/hsp/subabuse99/subabuse.htm.

U.S. General Accounting Office. (1994). GOA/HEHS-94-89: *Foster Care: Parental Drug Abuse Has Alarming Impact on Young Children.* Washington, DC: Author. Available online at http://161.203.16.4/t2pbat3/151435.pdf.

Wang, C. & Daro, D. (1997). *Current Trends in Child Abuse Reporting and Fatalities: The Results of the 1996 Annual Fifty State Survey.* Chicago, IL: National Center on Child Abuse Prevention Research, National Committee to Prevent Child Abuse.

Wallace, J. (1985). *Drug addiction: New light on the disease.* Chapel Hill, NC: Lexis Press.

Wegscheider, S. (1981). *Another chance: Hope and health for the drug addict family.* Palo Alto, CA: Science and Behavior Books.

Weiner, I. B. (1980). *Psychopathology in adolescence.* New York: Wiley.

Woititz, J. G. (1983). *Adult children of drug addicts.* Deerfield Beach, FL: Health Communications, Inc.

Wolin, S. J., Bennett, L. A., & Noonan, D. L. (1979). Family rituals and the recurrence of alcoholism over generations. *American Journal of Psychiatry, 136,* 589–593.

Wolin, S., & Wolin, S. (1993). *The resilient self.* New York: Villard Books.

Wolock, I. & Magura, S. (1996). Parental Substance Abuse as a Predictor of Child Maltreatment Re-reports, *Child Abuse & Neglect 20,* 1183–1193.

Young, N. K., Gardner, S.L., & Dennis, K. (1998). *Responding to alcohol and other drug problems in child welfare: Weaving together practice and policy.* Washington, DC: Child Welfare League of America.

Youngs, B. (1985). *Stress in children: How to recognize, avoid and overcome it.* New York: Arbor House.

Bibliography and *Suggested Reading
Child Welfare

Brohl, K. (2004). *The new miracle workers: Overcoming contemporary challenges in child welfare work.* Washington, DC: CWLA Press.

U.S. General Accounting Office. (1998). GAO/HEHS-98-182: *Foster care: Agencies face challenges securing stable homes for children of substance abusers.* Washington, DC: Author. Available online at http://www.gao.gov/atext/d03626t.txt

Children and Adolescents

* Arnold, L. (1978). *Helping parents help their children.* New York: Brunner/Mazel.

Bandura, A., & Walters, R. (1971). *Dependency in child development: A study of growth processes.* Itasca, IL: Peacock.

Bandura, A., & Walters, R. H. (1963) Aggression. In H. W. Stevenson (Ed.), *Child psychology: Sixty-second yearbook of the National Society for the Study of Education.* (pp. 364–415). Chicago: University of Chicago Press.

* Bell, R. (1998). *Changing bodies, changing lives: A book for teens on sex and relationships* (Third Edition). New York: Random House.

Booth, R. E., & Zhang, Y. (1996). Severe aggression and related conduct problems among runaway and homeless adolescents. *Psychiatric Services, 47(1),* 75–80.

* Bower, T. G. R. (1977). *A primer of infant development.* San Francisco: W.F. Freeman.

* Chess, S., Thomas, A., & Birch, H. (1976). *Your child is a person: A psychological approach to parenting without guilt.* New York: Penguin Books.

* Crowe, B. (1980). Living with a toddler. Boston: George Allen and Unwin.

Demone, H., & Weschler, H. (1976). Changing drinking patterns of adolescents since the 1960s. In M. Greenblatt & M. Shuckit (Eds.), Drug addiction problems in women and children. New York: Grune and Stratton.

Dugan, T., & Coles, R. (1989). *The child in our times: Studies in the development of resiliency.* New York: Brunner/Mazel.

* Gardner, R. (1982). *The boys and girls book about step-families.* New York: Bantam.

* Ginott, H. (1965). *Between parent and child.* New York: MacMillan.

* Ginott, H. (1969). *Between parent and teenager.* New York: MacMillan.

* Kolodny, R., Kolodny, N., Bratter, T., & Deep, C. (1984). How to survive your adolescent's adolescence. Boston: Little Brown.

Morrow, W., & Robert, W. (1961). Family relations of bright high achieving and underachieving high school boys. *Child Develop nent, 32(50/10).*

* Missildine, W. (1963). *Your inner child of the past.* New York: Pocket Books.

* Schaefer, C. (1982). *How to influence children: A complete guide for becoming a better parent.* New York: Van Nostrand Reinhold.

* Youngs, B. (1985). *Stress in children: How to recognize, avoid and overcome it.* New York: Arbor House.

Children of Drug Addicts

* Ackerman, R. J. (1983). *Children of drug addicts: A guidebook for educators, therapists, and parents* (2nd ed.). Holmes Beach, FL: Learning.

* Al-Anon Family Groups. (1979). *How can I help my children?* New York: Author.

* Al-Anon Family Groups. (1980). *Alateen: Hope for children of drug addicts.* New York: Author.

Anthony, E. J., & Cohler, B. (1987). *The invulnerable child.* New York: Guilford.

* Black, C. (1981). *It will never happen to me.* Denver, CO: Medical Administration.

* Black, C. (1985). *Repeat after me: Workbook for adult children.* Denver, CO: Medical Administration.

* Cermak, T. A. (1985). *Primer on adult children of drug addicts.* Deerfield Beach, FL: Health Communications.

Children of Alcoholics Foundation. (1990). *Children of alcoholics in the medical system: Hidden problems, hidden costs.* New York: Author.

Fitzgerald, H. E., Sullivan, L. A. Ham, H. P. Zucker, R. A. Bruckel, S. Schneider, A. M., et al. (1993). Predictors of behavior problems in three-year-old sons of alcoholics: Early evidence for the onset of risk. *Child Development, 4*, 110–123.

Friel, J., Subby, R., & Friel, L. (1984). *Co-dependency and the search for identity.* Deerfield Beach, FL: Health Communications.

Garmezy, N., & Rutter, M. (1988). *Stress, coping and development in children.* Baltimore: Johns Hopkins University Press.

Goodwin, D., Schulsinger, F., Hermansen, L., Guze, S., & Winokur, G. (1973). Drug addict problems in adoptees raised apart from drug addict biological parents. *Archives of General Psychiatry, 28*, 238–243.

* Gravitz, H. L., & Bowden, J. D. (1985). *Guide to recovery: A book for adult children of drug addicts.* Holmes Beach, FL: Learning.

* Greenleaf, J. (1981). *Co-drug addict, para-drug addicts.* Los Angeles, CA: Jael Greenleaf.

Jackson, J. K. (1954). The adjustment of the family to the crises of drug addiction. *Quarterly Journal of Studies on Alcohol, 15*, 562–586.

* Kritsberg, W. (1986). *The adult children of drug addicts syndrome: From discovery to recovery.* Deerfield Beach, FL.: Health Communications, Inc.

Nardi, P. M. (1981). Children of drug addicts: A role-theoretical perspective. Journal of Social Psychology, 115, 237–245.

Oliver-Diaz, P., & Slotwinski, J. (1984). Helping children to help themselves. *Focus on Family and Chemical Dependency, 7*(2), 36–37.

Oliver-Diaz, P. (1985). Teenage co-dependents: The chemical is not the issue. *Focus on Family and Chemical Dependency, 8*(1), 17–19.

* Wegscheider, S. (1981). *Another chance: Hope and health for the drug addict family.* Palo Alto, CA: Science and Behavior Books.

* Whitfield, C. (1987). *Healing the child within.* Deerfield Beach, FL: Health Communications, Inc.

Wilson, C., & Oxford, J. (1978). Children of drug addicts: Report of a preliminary study and comments on the literature. *Journal of Studies on Alcohol, 39*(1), 121–142.

Woititz, J. G. (1983). *Adult children of drug addicts.* Deerfield Beach, FL: Health Communications, Inc.

* Woititz, J. G. (1985). *The struggle for intimacy.* Deerfield Beach, FL: Health Communications, Inc.

Drug Addiction

*Al-Anon Family Groups. (2001). *Alcoholics Anonymous.* New York: Author.

* Al-Anon Family Groups. (2004). *Twelve steps and twelve traditions.* New York: Author.

Children's Defense Fund. (1998). *Healing the whole family: A look at family care programs.* Washington, DC: Author.

* Milam, J., & Ketcham, K. (1981). *Under the influence.* Seattle, WA: Madrona.

O'Gorman, P. (1974, October). Alcoholism, the family disease. *Urban Health, Journal of Health Care in the Cities,* Special Edition: Public Health.

Pace, N., & Ketcham, K. (2009). *Teens under the influence: The truth about kids, alcohol, and other drugs.* New York: Ballantine Books.

Russell, M. (1982). The epidemiology of alcohol-related birth defects. In E. L. Abel (Ed.), *Fetal alcohol syndrome, Vol. 2: Human Studies* (pp. 89–126). Boca Raton, FL: CRC Press.

Eating Disorders

* Hollis, J. (1985). *Fat is a family affair.* Minneapolis, MN: Hazelden.

Hood, J., Moore, T. E., & Garner, D. M. (1982). Locus of control as a measure of ineffectiveness in anorexia nervosa. *Journal of Consulting and Clinical Psychology, 50,* 3–13.

Schwartz, R. C., Barrett, M. J., & Saba, G. (1985). Family therapy for bulimia. In D. M. Garner & P. E Garfinkel (Eds.), *Handbook for psychotherapy for anorexia nervosa and bulimia* (pp. 280–307). New York: Guilford.

Gambling

Blaszczynski, A. (1985, December). A winning bet: Treatment for compulsive gambling. *Psychology Today.*

Blaszczynski, A. (1985, May). Brain chemistry and the gambler's high. *Psychology Today.*

Holden, C. (1985, December 12). Against all odds. *Psychology Today, 19,* 31-36.

Resilience

Seligman, M. (1995). *The optimistic child.* New York: Houghton Mifflin.

Werner, E., & Smith, R. (1992). *Overcoming the odds.* Ithaca, NY: Cornell University Press.

Trauma and Posttraumatic Stress Disorder

* Bass, E., & Davis, L. (1998). *The courage to heal: A guide for women survivors of child sexual abuse.* New York: Harper and Row.

Black, C., Bucky, S., & Wilder-Padilla, S. (1986). The interpersonal and emotional consequences of being an adult child of a drug addict. *International Journal of the Addictions, 21,* 213–231.

Courtois, C. A. (1988). *Healing the incest wound: Adult survivors in therapy.* New York: W.W. Norton.

Evans, K., & Sullivan, J. (1995). *Treating addicted survivors of trauma.* New York: Guilford.

Green, B. L. (1988). *Trauma and its wake: The study and treatment of posttraumatic stress disorder.* New York: Brunner/Mazel.

Ochberg, F. (1988). *Post-traumatic therapy and victims of violence.* New York: Brunner/Mazel.

Peterson, K., Prout, M., & Schwarz, R. (1992). *Post-traumatic stress disorder: A clinician's guide.* New York: Plenum Press.

About the Authors

Dr. Patricia O'Gorman is a psychologist, consultant, and author noted for her work in the child welfare and substance abuse fields where she has pio-
neered strength-based approaches. She is currently
Chief Psychologist of Berkshire Farm Center, in
Canaan, NY. She has held the positions of Director
of the Division of Prevention for the National
Institute of Alcohol Abuse and Alcoholism, Found-
ing Director of the National Council on Alcoholism's Department of Prevention
and Education, and cofounder of the National Association of Children of Alcoholics. Dr. O'Gorman was also a faculty member of New York University's School
of Medicine, Department of Psychiatry. She has lectured both nationally and
internationally and is known for her funny, high-energy presentations. She has
appeared on TV shows such as *Good Morning America*, *The Today Show*, and *AM
Sunday*, and is also the author of seven books in the recovery/self-help field, including *Dancing Backwards in High Heels: How Women Master the Art of Resilience* and *The Clinical Program Model of The Berkshire Model of Care and
Treatment...of roots and of wings...*

Dr. O'Gorman lives in New York State with her husband, Robert Ross, and her
sons, Jeremy and Mike.

 **Philip Diaz, MSW,** is currently the CEO of Gateway Community Services, Inc., the largest provider of substance abuse treatment and prevention services for adults, children, and families in northeast Florida. A social worker with over 25 years of experience in drug prevention and treatment, Mr. Diaz has been nationally recognized for his pioneering work with women and children in the area of substance abuse and child welfare.

As the former Assistant Deputy Director for Prevention in the Office of Demand Reduction within the White House Office of National Drug Control Policy, Phil was the lead federal official in the development of national and international drug prevention policy. He is a founding board m :mber of the National Association for Children of Alcoholics and the National Association of Native American Children of Alcoholics, and founding chairperson of the National Drug Prevention League. He has served as a Special Consultant to D.A.R.E. America, the Drug Enforcement Administration's Center for Substance Abuse Prevention, and the Executive Office of the President. An internationally known lecturer, Mr. Diaz has trained around the United States and in Australia. His work has appeared in *Women's Day Magazine, USA Today,* and *Focus on the Family.*

Mr. Diaz received his MSW from Fordham University and his BA from City College of New York. He was awarded an Honorary Doctorate of Law from Mercy College. Mr. Diaz lives in Jacksonville, Florida, with his wife, author Kathryn Brohl, and their cat, Shakti.

Pat and Phil have collaborated for over 20 years and authored four books together: *Breaking the Cycle of Addiction: 12 Steps to Self-Parenting* (Health Communications, 1987); *Self-Parenting 12-Step Workbook: Windows to Your Inner Child* (Health Communications, 1990); *12 Steps to Self-Parenting* (Health Communications, 1991); and *The Lowdown on Families Who Get High: Successful Parenting for Families Affected by Addiction.* They can be reached at www.ogormandiaz.com.